WISH WE KNEW WHAT TO SAY

Also by Pragya Agarwal

Sway: Unravelling Unconscious Bias

WISH WE KNEW WHAT TO SAY

TALKING WITH CHILDREN ABOUT RACE

PRAGYA AGARWAL

dialogue
books

DIALOGUE BOOKS

First published in Great Britain in 2020 by Dialogue Books

10 9 8 7 6 5 4 3 2 1

A CIP catalogue record for this book
is available from the British Library.

ISBN 978-0-349-70205-6

Typeset in Berling by M Rules
Printed and bound in Great Britain by Clays Ltd, Elcograf S.p.A.

Papers used by Dialogue Books are from well-managed forests
and other responsible sources.

Dialogue Books
An imprint of
Little, Brown Book Group
Carmelite House
50 Victoria Embankment
London EC4Y 0DZ

An Hachette UK Company
www.hachette.co.uk

www.littlebrown.co.uk

For all those who have fought and resisted
And those who stood by their side

CONTENTS

Section IV: Four to Six Years

Section V: Seven to Nine Years

Section VI: Ten to Twelve Years

INTRODUCTION

We live in a multicultural diverse society, but race is still a very sensitive topic to talk about. Few parents would consider themselves or their children racist, with its connotations of intentional, angry or mean behaviour against different groups of people. But even when we are not intentionally racist, we can make judgements based on skin colour and perceived race, and act in a prejudicial way. Race is such an ingrained social construct that we can never truly dissociate ourselves from it: people are socially conditioned to assign values to someone based on their skin colour.

Born in India and having lived in the UK for two decades, I am guilty of ignoring my own racial heritage and roots. For too long, I tried to fit in. I wanted to be known for my achievements and not because I look different, and I wanted to avoid any racial biases, any suggestions of brown privilege or any stereotypical associations.

And so I avoided talking about my race altogether.

But in doing so, I also avoided a conversation about race and race politics with my eldest child (I'll refer to her as P) who was born in India and was brought up here in the UK. And I know many other immigrant parents who have done the same.

Since the birth of my twins, I have become increasingly conscious of this. They are dual-heritage and they do not look like me or their older sister. I started looking at the books that we have been reading with them, and could not find many characters of colour. Diversity in children's literature is a huge concern and research suggests that over 80 per cent of characters in children's books are white.

In 2018 only 4 per cent of children's books published in the UK had a minority ethnic hero. The survey included all new books for children aged between three and eleven. The proportion is an increase on 2017, when just 1 per cent of main characters were BAME.[1] In 2018, 42 per cent of children's books published in the UK had animals or inanimate objects as main characters, meaning that a reader from a BAME background is much more likely to encounter a book where an animal is the main character than they are to encounter a book that contains a character who shares their ethnicity or cultural heritage.

This doesn't reflect the reality of our world. It does not allow my children to look beyond stereotypes, to understand that their view is never less (or more) important than that of someone who is not the same skin colour as theirs, that they are no less important than someone who has blonde hair and blue eyes – the stereotype character in children's books and in the media.

By dismissing or keeping silent about our race and others', we reinforce the notion that people are not born equal, and allow children to make their own judgement and inferences about racial equality. By saying that 'everyone is the same' we deny our children their own racial and cultural experiences. We also dismiss the fact that racism is still a huge problem in many parts of this world, and we whitewash many significant events of racial crime and segregation in history.

Research both in the US and the UK has found that non-immigrant white parents mainly discussed race in response to a race-related incident. Often white parents shirk it from fear of getting it wrong or not having the right vocabulary. Some feel that children are naturally unbiased and that race is not a relevant feature for them to talk about, such as these experiences that parents have shared in a recent workshop that I did:

'We only use clothing colours or hair colour to describe or differentiate between people. It has never occurred to him that anyone is different. I really like that they don't seem to notice skin colour.'

'I have always told my child that everyone is equal, and that skin colour makes no difference.'

Some parents believe that if their child goes to a diverse school or lives in a diverse community, and plays with children from different backgrounds, there is no need to talk about race or racism, as the child does not notice difference. Parents often assume that their child is unbiased if they have not said anything.

A study published in 2016[2] analysed data gathered from 107 white American mothers raising white children aged four to seven years. It is not just a mother's responsibility to talk about race and racism with their children. In this study, there were initially 144 participants. However, due to the low number of fathers, the sample was reduced to the mothers for the purpose of uniformity. Also, they excluded the 11 parents who were raising mixed-race children, as in these families race is much more salient and therefore most mothers believed that the topic was important to discuss. Only 30 per cent were categorised as having a colour-conscious approach, whereas 70 per cent indicated a colour-blind approach, presuming that their silence would lead children to not notice differences and thus remain unbiased. Many also indicated that they would only approach it if an issue came up or if the child asked questions.

It is not only white parents who can raise children with prejudice, or are guilty of prejudice. This is a false assumption, because we all have this capacity. The responsibilities run across the board for both white parents and parents of colour. All parents need to prepare kids for intolerance, and all parents need to prepare kids for being appreciative of other people. All parents need to be prepared to address racial prejudice and racism. For us parents of colour, we need to make sure we don't ignore individual responsibility when we talk to our children about systemic and structural racial biases and prejudices. As an Indian parent, I have to actively counter the anti-blackness that is so deeply embedded in many Asian communities, and the erasure of black history in our education. If I don't do this actively and vocally, then I am enabling anti-blackness.

We live in a multicultural world.[3] But there is still racial inequity, and consequences of racism and racial inequality are real. For example, an experiment[4] by the sociologist Devah Pager showed how race affects hiring. The researchers sent out one black and one white person to apply for 350 jobs in New York City with identical CVs. They were given identical scripts and were even dressed alike. The black applicant got half the call-backs that the white applicant got. There were no differences in merit. Race was the cause. A study in 2018 showed the continuing existence of discrimination in the housing market against applicants whose surnames suggest that they are minority ethnic individuals, who on average have to send out more applications than those whose last names suggest they are of the majority white population. Merely on the basis of a typical minority ethnic surname, the landlord often infers that an applicant is likely to be in a weaker financial position than other applicants.

In Australia,[5] for instance, more than 34 per cent of children have both parents born overseas. A project carried out by Western Sydney University, *Challenging Racism*, has found a high level of racial discrimination. More than 75 per cent of the 6,001 people surveyed in 2016 said that immigrants should assimilate rather than maintain their own traditions. More than 34 per cent had experienced racism in workplaces, on public transport and in educational institutions. 27.6 per cent of respondents indicated that they would be 'extremely' or 'very' concerned if a relative were to marry a Muslim. 63 per cent of respondents expressed some degree (ranging from slight to extreme) of intolerance/discomfort with Muslim Australians. 51.4 per cent expressed anti-Middle Eastern sentiment, and 43.9 per cent of respondents expressed anti-African sentiment. Almost 14 per cent of the people self-identified as racist or having prejudiced views, who were found to be the hardcore far-right extremists. But racial prejudice is not carried just by such people who might engage in more explicit hate crimes. It is the everyday racism, the implicit biases, that we all can be guilty of carrying with us.

I do not believe that parenting works with a template-based approach. As a parent of a grown-up daughter, and now of four-year-old twins, I know that every child differs, and parenting each child even in the same home takes a completely different approach. Children have different sensibilities, and different responses to what they see around them. It would be naïve of me to recommend this book as a step-by-step guide to be followed rigidly. My frustration with many of the parenting books is that they consider these age boundaries to be so rigid, and if a parent's child is different, I know how much stress and anxiety it can cause them to feel that their child does not fit the milestones, does not conform to the norm. Therefore, even as I break things down as per age, I want parents to take these as flexible, only as a tentative guide.

Much of our behaviour cannot fit into neat categories even as we try and make it for ease of managing conversations around childhood behaviour. You know best as a parent if your child is ready for a conversation or not, but it is also worth remembering that sometimes our parenting bias prevents us from approaching seemingly difficult subjects with our children because we worry about their reaction, we do not wish to sully their innocence and their faith in the goodness of this world, we want to protect them from any ugliness within it. But our children can surprise us. We have to honour our children's interest and curiosity from a young age, and understand that they are often far more intelligent and resilient than we give them credit for.

Children can really only grow up completely non-racist if they grow up in a non-racist world, where race as a social construct does not matter, where the colour of the skin does not afford anyone privileges or put up barriers. But this is not the case really, is it? Children pick up social cues and messages from all around them. This is why our role as a parent, a carer, an educator, becomes even more crucial. A lot of parenting is unlearning the internalised racism that we may have absorbed through our own upbringing. Children are watching us, observing us. No parenting is apolitical. We cannot just introduce diverse books and media. We also have to model these behaviours and dismantle and contest racism and ingrained biases in our own words and actions.

Sometimes when we as parents have faced racism in our lives, we can carry that trauma with us, and that can also affect our parenting. We can teach our children through unconscious cues to be less open about who they are, lest it leads to prejudice or discrimination, or we can teach them to be afraid of differences and anyone who does not look like them. Some of the unconscious stereotypes we carry are transferred through our actions, words, gestures, without us even meaning to. Raising children who are comfortable with race is also raising more courageous and open children, open to difference and open to new and diverse experiences.

We are also giving our children crucial critical thinking skills that are so important, especially right now as they are bombarded with information from all sides.

As parents, either we can choose to be proactive, where we introduce race and racism from a young age and actively talk about it in order to raise colour-conscious children, or we can take a reactive approach where we only talk about these things when our children mention something. The latter is the colour-blind approach that I will discuss further later in the book. The former approach works better.

In telling our children that 'race does not matter' and in raising children to be colour-blind, we are actually creating more harm than good. We are not educating our children in the way racial inequalities work, and we are telling them that what a person of colour may go through is not valid. And we are dismissing their experience. We are not teaching our children that they may have certain privileges because of their skin colour, and in failing to do so we are making them less socially aware and empathetic towards those who do not have the same privileges. When we do not talk about race and identity actively, children are more likely to internalise any racism, and form a negative view of themselves; they are more likely to pick up stereotypes about people and incorrectly judge them; and they can be unsure of how to tackle any racially charged words and actions targeted at them or others around them.

Saying 'we don't see colour' does not equate to meaning 'we are not racist'. It is not enough to merely tell our children that everyone is equal. We have to be actively anti-racist, particularly as they are growing up in a society where nationalistic identities and politics are increasingly taking centre stage. We are not all of us the same, we are all unique individuals, and every child has to know and understand this. We are different, and still we are equal. No one should be treated differently or have different rights and privileges just because of their skin colour, or their racial category. Saying this to children would actually make them feel more comfortable in their own identity and their own uniqueness. And that strong sense of self-identity is really important for a child's mental and physical well-being.

Data projections in the UK suggest that minority ethnic people will make up a larger proportion of the population in the future, and the numerical significance of those claiming a mixed or multiple heritage in particular is set to increase if current trends continue. A 2015 Pew research study[6] (21,224 sample size with 1,555 multiracial adults) found that multiracial babies accounted for 10 per cent of births in the United States in 2013, up from 1 per cent in 1970. This is taking into account that it was only around 50 years ago that the US Supreme Court, in the case bearing the evocative title *Loving v. Virginia* (1967), struck down laws prohibiting mixed-race marriages. And it has been only 15 years since the US Census Bureau first allowed Americans to choose more than one race when filling out their census form. This survey also found that those biracial adults who are both white and black are three times as likely to say they have a lot in common with people who are black than with those who are white (58 vs 19 per cent). They also feel more accepted by blacks than by whites, and report having far more contact with their black relatives. 69 per cent say they've had a lot of contact with family members who are black over the course of their lives, while just 21 per cent report similar levels of contact with their white relatives. About 41 per cent say they have had no contact with family members who are white. One in four of the adults surveyed said that people are often confused by their racial background, and a majority (55 per cent) say they have been subjected to racial slurs or jokes.

Even as these figures show why we need to talk about race or racism, I am aware that this can be problematic in itself because it contributes to the performative aspects of talking about racism.

Mixed-race adults often straddle two or more worlds, and their experiences and relationships reflect that. I know from my own experience of two children who are mixed-race (for want of a better term) that such 'mixedness' can be messy and complicated when trying to form a sense of identity. Whether it's in books, articles, films, plays, documentaries, academic journals or even threads on Twitter, we are continuously reminded of the plight of 'mixed-race' people coming to terms with their divided identity. And I believe that we need to re-examine how mixedness is narrated and lived within our communities and institutions without stereotyping mixed-race or multiracial people in the process. They are not a homogeneous faceless mass, united by their sense of mixedness, the inherent messiness inbuilt in this vocabulary, but instead each forms their own unique identity, a true reflection of the multicultural society that we are living in. Nevertheless, their proximity to whiteness becomes a privilege as well as a barrier to realising their true racialised realities. I will discuss this more later on in the book.

In talking openly about race and racial justice, we are helping our children understand that even though our history has shaped certain power imbalances and we are all part of this system, they have the power to break some of these cycles, that they can readdress these imbalances, and that they can feel empowered to make positive change. In helping our children claim their racial identities we address some of the stereotypes that can form through learned socialisations and catch them before they start becoming deeply rooted. In helping our children understand racism and racial prejudice, we help them understand that they are neither victims nor villains, and they are free to be proud of who they truly are without having to hide parts of themselves.

Various studies, including those from the American Academy of Pediatrics (AAP), have recently started to focus more closely on the impact of racism and racial trauma on children's health, even as this has long been ignored. The impact of racism has been linked to birth disparities and mental health problems in children and adolescents, from low birth rate to sleep disorders, stress and anxiety. The AAP President Dr Sara Goza says that: 'Racism harms children's health, starting from before they are born. A growing body of research supports this, and we cannot ignore the impact.' The biological mechanism that emerges from chronic stress leads to increased and prolonged levels of exposure to stress hormones and oxidative stress at the cellular level. Prolonged exposure to stress hormones such as cortisol leads to inflammatory reactions that predispose individuals to chronic disease. The AAP also shows that it is not just those who directly experience racism who suffer the side-effects, but also the bystanders. This means that even if your children are unlikely to ever suffer any racism themselves, they can still pick up trauma-related stress and anxiety from observing their friends or other schoolchildren being a target, or even from the racial incidents they read about or watch on the news. This is a powerful reminder of why even as a white parent, you have a responsibility to discuss race and racism openly with your children and to give them the necessary tools for both countering and tackling racism.

This book is not meant just for white parents. We all need to discuss race and racism with our children, no matter what our and their ethnic background is, as it is a determinant of our and their identities, and of their sense of belonging. While white parents might have the privilege of not having this conversation with their children because there is no urgent need to do so, parents of colour, and with children of mixed race, have to strike up these conversations, as it is more likely for these children to stand out and be bullied in the playground, to be discriminated against for the way they look. In either case, our children are forming their own and others' racial identities, internalising racism, and creating a sense of social hierarchy and their own place in it, which will shape how they make friends, who they make friends and form relationships with, what kind of self-image they have, and how they treat others around them. It is not merely about kindness and compassion for others, although that matters. It is about children's own self-identities, and giving them the ability to create their own stories and narratives rather than letting others impose these upon them. It is allowing them to flourish with a strong sense of self, whatever their racial identity may be. And in doing so, we are not telling them to ignore their own or other children's ethnic and cultural identities, but to recognise and acknowledge differences and know how to tackle them in a fair and equitable manner.

This book assembles the science behind the way that children form their sense of self- and racial identities, which is as relevant for white parents as for parents of colour and those with children with mixed heritage. I supplement this with my own experience of raising my three children. Each section includes questions that other parents have asked me along the way in my various workshops and talks. These questions may be the ones that your children ask you too, but, more importantly, they can be used to anticipate the things that children are thinking about, and those that can be stepping stones to first conversations around race and racism. Some of these conversations will be difficult, as you try to unravel the way that whiteness and racism get embedded in our places and in our family structures, often purposefully silenced and/or enabled through misinformation and ignorance. But unless we sit with discomfort and help our children do the same, real change will not happen.

I focus on early years because these are really the most crucial. Often any anti-racism work that is done in schools is focused on adolescents, and often parents think that children are too young to tackle complex concepts such as race and racism. But research shows that by the time children are six years old they already have well-formed attitudes that mainly stem from their environment and parents. By the age of nine, many of the racial stereotypes have been laid down very firmly and have grown harder to dislodge. Thus, by the time parents perceive their children to be old enough, the children's attitudes may already be well established and more resistant to change.

Early teacher–child interactions are important for long-term academic outcomes, but often these interactions can be affected by racism and implicit bias. We know from research that children of colour, especially black children, can receive worse assessments from their teachers, and more often be picked upon and penalised for bad behaviour. The social environment that children are raised in affects their development and their health, offers our children the necessary tools to navigate this messily racialised world, and gives them an immunity from racial prejudice, an intentionality to uphold social justice values, and the superpower to change the world as they grow up. Now, doesn't that sound beautiful? I think it really does.

If we want our children to thrive and flourish in a diverse, multicultural world, we owe it to them to help them make sense of the confusing and emotionally charged messages they receive about themselves and others. We owe it to our children to work together to instil pride in their heritage and culture, and an unshakeable sense of self-worth and identity. This is how they will learn to support each other, and to stand up to injustice and inequality. When we give our children the tools and vocabulary to talk about people's differences and similarities in an open, non-judgemental, inquisitive way, we can help them address any unfairness they may see or encounter. Yes, it can be unsettling to do so, but in enabling our children to step outside their comfort zones, we support critical thinking in our children and prepare them for a more demanding relationship with their world, as the author Jamaica Kincaid says:

> And might not knowing why they are the way they are, why they do the things they do, why they live the way they live and in the place they live, why the things that happened to them happened, lead ... people to a different relationship with the world, a more demanding relationship ...?

These are the people who are going to inherit this world, and we owe it to them to lay a strong foundation for the next phases of their lives.

I would recommend starting at the very start here, no matter how old your child is. Because you have to lay a strong foundation before you start to build the structure.

Pragya Agarwal
July 2020

Section I

What Does It Mean?

First of all, we need to help our children build a strong vocabulary around race and racism. Many of these are highly nuanced terms, and we don't want to fall at the first hurdle of having to explain them to our children.

RACE

Race as a social construct is rooted in history and remains a mechanism through which society has been divided and controlled over time. We know that for a very long time science was used to justify race as a biological reality and to reinforce the notions of racial superiority, to validate the oppression of one group of people by another. Often skin colour or ancestry has been used as a demarcation for racial category, and we use labels such as 'black', 'white' and 'brown', but in reality there are no traits, no characteristics, not even one gene that is present in all members of one so-called race and absent in another. Dr Francis Collins, former director of the Human Genome Project and the director of the National Institutes of Health, has affirmed that humans are 99.9 per cent the same at the level of their genome.

The A, B and O blood groups can be found in all the world's population. For instance, the percentage of Estonians and Papua New Guineans with A, B and O blood is almost exactly identical. Skin colour tends to correspond with the local prevalence of ultraviolet radiation from the sun and hence with geographic latitude, so that people with ancestors from the tropics typically have darker skin while those further north have lighter skin. Sub-Saharan Africans, Asian Indians, Aboriginal Australians and Melanesians all have dark skin. But skin colour really does not determine any other traits, such as intelligence or athleticism. Most traits are inherited independently from one another. The genes that influence skin colour have nothing to do with those that influence hair form, eye shape and blood type, let alone with the far more complex traits we value such as intelligence, musical ability or athletic ability. Genetic diseases are inherited through families, not race.

We are all Africans. Modern humans (*Homo sapiens*) originated in Africa, and we spent most of our evolution as a species together there. Some modern humans first left Africa around 50,000 to 70,000 years ago and spread out around the world. All the other populations of the world can be seen as a subset of Africans. Every human genetic trait found elsewhere can also be found in Africa, with the exception of relatively few recent variations, such as lighter skin.

Beneath the skin colour, we are all the same biologically. We may categorise people as white, black or brown, but these visual variations don't accurately reflect the genetic differences – or rather similarities – between us.

All the same, these artificial constructs that have been imposed upon humans mean that people have used them to oppress some groups of people: this history and legacy of oppression has created a system of profound disadvantage for some such groups that manifests as racism. We cannot understand the notions of race and racism outside the context of history, and without learning why this misguided belief in biological difference underpinning racial categories was designed to justify the superiority of one race – a socially constructed group – over another. This is why children have to be taught history that communicates this important message of why these racial labels and categories exist, and how these contribute to racism today.

The science of race is as important as understanding our history. History tells us how society laid down racial lines, which has led to systemic and structural inequities. Science shows us the biological understanding of race, and how pseudoscience contributes to myth. Genetic analysis can show people from the Caribbean have Asian ancestry, or African Americans have European ancestry. This can help children understand that how people are identified is determined by society and not always based on their genetics or biology.

Race is a social construct. It is not real. But the impact of race is very real.

RACISM

Racism is a system of disadvantage that is in place because certain ethnicities are incorrectly considered superior to others by some people. And children will experience it. Matthew Clair and Jeffrey S. Denis define it in their 'Sociology of Racism' as 'individual- and group-level processes and structures that are implicated in the reproduction of racial inequality'.

Bias is a conscious or unconscious prejudice against an individual or group based on their identity. And racism can result from such biases due to racial identity, when such beliefs result into action.

There are three levels through which racism operates: individual, systemic and institutional. I discuss these in detail in the last section of the book.

Children can experience implicit or explicit individual and interpersonal racism as well as suffer the consequence of systemic and institutional racism depending on where they live, where they study, what their economic status is. Children can internalise the individual racism, and the stereotypes of their own racial groups. Children can contribute to, support, and enable interpersonal racism, by active racial prejudice and bullying or by being a silent bystander.

Systemic or structural racism happens when there is inherent inequality in the structures or processes carried out by groups with power, such as governments, businesses or schools.

For instance, in South Africa, during the colonial times, the Dutch East India Company introduced racial segregation. In 1795 the British took over the Cape of

Good Hope, and they continued with racial segregation, which became a particularly explosive idea during the apartheid period. Race was used for political, social and economic purposes. During this period from 1948, the government introduced numerous legislations based on racial classification. For example, the Population Registration Act divided the South African population into four main racial groups: Whites, Natives (Blacks), Indians and Coloured people (people of mixed race). Politically, White people had the rights to vote, access to state security and protection as well as representation in the National Assembly, the privilege of having access to much more skilled and office jobs, and they had access to own the productive land and other means of productions. The Bantu Education Act of 1953 legalised racial separation of education in South Africa, and so a separate system of education was designed for black South African students which was in essence designed to prepare black people for lives as a labouring class. Existing universities were not permitted to enrol new black students. Although the apartheid era ended in 1994, and the country is now, as per its constitution, committed to ensuring redress for past racially discriminatory policies, these long years of discriminatory practices mean that black people never had the same opportunities and resources. This means that implicit and subversive racism exists, and systemic and structural inequalities continue to persist. The effects of racism are seen long beyond when explicit racism has ended. And this is why children have to understand that our current positions of power and privilege are often shaped by our histories of oppression, and that history shapes who still faces racism and discrimination today.

Racism has significant adverse effects on any child who receives, commits or observes it. This is why creating diverse environments and advocating for racial justice not only benefits those who are more likely to suffer from racism due to their membership of a minority ethnic community, but also those children who have the advantage of being white, or belong to the majority community.

And this is why a positive racial identity is crucial for the healthy development of all children as they enter adolescence.

ETHNICITY

When people are asked to define their identity, it can be tricky to know how to narrow it down. I often wonder whether it is my nationality, my country of birth or my family's ancestry. People often define their identity by race, especially in places and societies where racialisation has created these strong divides.

Ethnicity is a person's identity based on their cultural

heritage. Often ethnicity is a form of kinship connecting people based on common characteristics of ancestry, territorial possession, language, forms of dress, a sense of history and religion. It is considered an anthropological term because it is based on learned behaviours. In South Africa, for instance, the different ethnic groups were derived from different rural homelands, grounded in different cultural practices and perspectives.

Race and ethnicity are often used interchangeably, but technically they are two different things, even though neither has links to the human genome. While race is assigned externally by others, ethnicity is based on cultural roots and can be used to define self-identity. Often ethnicity is an easier way to identify ourselves when we associate membership with many different groups, such as Irish Indian, British Nigerian or African American. This allows people to ascribe their identity to cultural origins rather than be pigeonholed on the basis of physical characteristics.

It is very tricky to disentangle race and ethnicity, and people may find themselves being given a racial identity in society that overrides their ethnicity. For instance, a person coming from the Indian subcontinent might identify as being Indian, Tamil, Bengali, Bangladeshi, Pakistani or Nepali, based on language or national identities, but they are very likely to be all seen as 'brown' or 'Asian' in the UK or US first and foremost. Race therefore seems to be based on sociological categorisation, and is more explicit, while ethnicity is more cultural, flexible, and can be broadened.

Dalton Conley, Professor of Sociology at Princeton University, in speaking to PBS[7] argues that ethnicity is more fluid and crosses racial lines. He says: 'I have a friend who was born in Korea to Korean parents, but as an infant, she was adopted by an Italian family in Italy. Ethnically, she feels Italian: She eats Italian food, she speaks Italian, she knows Italian history and culture. She knows nothing about Korean history and culture. But when she comes to the United States, she's treated racially as Asian.'

In the 2010 census, 94 per cent of the US population selected one or more of the five government-defined 'racial categories': white, black, Asian, American Indian or Pacific Islander. It has been debated whether these are ethnic or racial categories. However, what was noticeable was that amongst the Latinos, just 63 per cent selected at least one of these categories. Out of 37 per cent of Latinos, or 18.5 million of the total 19 million who selected the 'other' option, many wrote their responses as 'Hispanic' or 'Latin American'. US Federal policy defines 'Hispanic' as an ethnicity and not a race, but these results from the census show that most Hispanic people consider their Hispanic background as part of their racial identity. It is also interesting that most multiracial Hispanic people do not consider themselves to be mixed-race. They have a strong sense of their identity and take pride in their heritage. There is ambivalence in the use of the term 'Hispanic' or 'Latino', and many prefer their country of origin such as 'Mexican' or 'Dominican' instead. The ongoing research carried out in the US by Pew Research Center has shown the multidimensional and complex nature of capturing racial identities, and how it can be often so reductive.

These labels and identities of course change and evolve over time. When Italian, Irish and Eastern European immigrants began to arrive in the United States, at first they were not considered part of the white race and were labelled as 'non-white immigrants', but then over time they became subcategories of the white race and ultimately assimilated into the broader label.

Such examples can help children understand how race is socially determined and can change over time, even though it is an identity that is imposed upon them by society and is the basis for the inequalities in our society. Using ethnicity for their self-identity can also help them assimilate multiple identities.

RACIALISATION

Racialisation is the process by which race, as a concept, becomes meaningful, and social and cultural meaning is assigned to it. The concept of race only really exists because of racialisation.

There are many definitions to it, but in summary what it results in is the organisation of people into hierarchies and power structures based on their perceived race membership. Racialisation is the process of 'essentialising', where everyone from a specific group is assigned a property that leads to homogenisation, and often dehumanisation, of the individuals.

There is a power imbalance in the way that racialisation works because historically it is something detrimental done to others as part of a power relationship. For instance, Frantz Fanon, writer of *Les Damnés de la Terre* (1961, translated as *The Wretched of the Earth* in 1963), attributes racialisation to the process of colonialisation, where European thought embodied the notion of whiteness as good and blackness as bad. Dehumanising the oppressed, and seeing them as a faceless mass, can absolve the oppressor of their guilt, and rationalise the oppression in terms of the oppressed being too weak and powerless to free or rule themselves.

While phenotype (observable physical properties such as appearance and behaviour) is an important marker in which groups get racialised in this process, often other aspects which are not as visible can be used for deciding these hierarchies. In the more recent past, the intersection of race and class has also created racialisation, as we have seen with the Irish in nineteenth-century Britain and the Eastern European Jews in early twentieth-century Europe. In Indian communities, for instance, casteism has been the basis of prejudice and social hierarchies for many centuries. So these racial divisions can go beyond the black–white binary, such as in the context of Latino immigrants, anti-Muslim sentiment, where religion has been used as a mechanism for racialisation, and prejudice against the traveller community.[8]

Anything that makes race or class a salient feature of social interaction and dynamics is racialisation. While most of racialisation is driven by oppression and subjugation, there have been instances of self-racialisation, such as the Black Power movement and the Black Lives Matter protests, which have deployed racialisation as an emancipatory act to overturn the existing narratives and create a positive identity and group solidarity.

Children can be supported in understanding how historic acts of racialisation have led to certain power imbalances and stereotyping of people based on race. This can help them understand different forms of oppression such as slavery and imperialism. Racialisation is not racism; rather it is the process by which racism is sustained. But internalised racism can also be prevented in children of colour by deploying racialisation to form a strong sense of racial identity and group solidarity, and to resist racism. This can be a very empowering message. I discuss it in detail later on in the book.

WHITE PRIVILEGE

Privilege comes from the Latin *privilegium*, meaning a law for just one person, a benefit enjoyed by an individual or group beyond what is available to others. As per the dictionary, it is 'a right, immunity, or benefit enjoyed only by a person beyond the advantages of most'.

When a person is born with a natural access to power and resources, it is difficult for them to notice their own privilege, but for those who do not have these advantages this privilege is very much visible. Those born with privilege just take it as normal, for granted. White privilege is something people are just naturally born with. It has nothing to do with whether they are a good person or not. Instead, it is a system of advantages conferred on a person due to their skin colour. Most important, people who are white are seen as individuals, while people of colour are mostly and almost always first viewed as part of a racial group.

White privilege is an institutional (rather than personal) set of benefits granted to those who, by race, resemble the people who dominate the powerful positions in our institutions. One of the primary privileges is that of having greater access to power and resources than people of colour do just because there are more white people as gatekeepers and decision-makers in our society. Studies in the National Bureau of Economic Research, for instance, show that a white person is ten times more likely to get a job as compared with a person of colour with a similar résumé, or more likely to get a loan approved. If white people are accused of a crime, they are less likely to be presumed guilty, less likely to be sentenced to death and more likely to be portrayed in a fair, nuanced manner by media outlets.

A few days ago, someone became very aggressive with me during one of my talks about white privilege. It wasn't the first time. They didn't think that they had any privileges and they listed a number of people of colour who were richer and more educated than they were. But white privilege does not mean that a person has not had any difficulties in their lives. It just means that they've not had the daily interruptions of casual racism, or faced discrimination based on their skin colour. Every person has a layer of privilege that they should acknowledge, things that give them a cushion and remove some obstruction from their path. White privilege is one such layer, a bubble wrap, a soft racism-proof bubble.

White privilege is not the lack of struggle. It is the absence of racism.

- It is switching on the TV and opening a magazine and seeing more people like yourself everywhere.
- It is not facing any discrimination and prejudice because of being in the minority, fearful of being stereotyped.
- It is being able to talk about racism without being seen as self-serving or even moany and whiny.
- It is being able to make decisions for everyone, without considering the views of those in the minority or thinking of involving them in the decision-making.
- It is being able to think of yourself as the norm.
- It is being able to dismiss lived experience of people of colour, with statements such as 'I don't think they meant any harm' or 'I don't think there is any racism in our society.'
- It is being able to centre yourself by statements such as 'I don't really think the issue is race as much as it is class.'
- It is being able to say and believe that 'Race is not my issue.'
- It is expecting people of colour to educate you on race and racism without doing the hard work yourself.
- It is having the luxury to not discuss racism with your children.

White privilege accords you a natural upper hand, a higher status in society because of the way our social norms are defined. It is knowing that you are and will always be the norm. So that is white privilege. It is a legacy as well as the cause of racism in our society. And not recognising or acknowledging it is the first sign of it.

DO YOU HAVE WHITE PRIVILEGE?

Some examples can include:

- ✔ If, until now, you have not thought much about race or racism, then you have white privilege.
- ✔ If you have never been followed around in a store by the security guard, or been racially profiled, you have white privilege.
- ✔ If you've never been on the receiving end of the assumption that when you've achieved something it's only because it was taken away from a white person who 'deserved it', you have white privilege.
- ✔ If no one has ever questioned your intellectual capabilities or attendance at an elite institution based solely on your skin colour, you have white privilege.
- ✔ If when taught about your national heritage or about civilisation, you are shown that people

of your skin colour/ethnicity made it what it is, then you have white privilege.

But white privilege is also so much more than this. It is the power to remain silent in the face of racial inequity and to avoid the discomfort and inconvenience that come with speaking up against racism. It is knowing that your status quo is safe, and your children will maintain their privileges and position in society.

We can make white privilege tangible and visible by using the analogy of an invisible backpack. Peggy McIntosh writes in *White Privilege: Unpacking the Invisible Knapsack* that: 'I was taught to see racism only in individual acts of meanness, not in invisible systems conferring dominance on my group'. Often it is easy to see racism and racial bias as something that is of disadvantage to other groups, but not to see how it is also enabled by a system that offers white people an advantage. Peggy describes white privilege as 'an invisible weightless knapsack of special provisions, maps, passports, codebooks, visas, clothes, tools, and blank checks'. This provides a vivid way of explaining white privilege to children without making them feel guilty for possessing this privilege, or like a victim for not having it. Children can understand how they use the privileges that they have. White privilege is one, but education, class and socio-economic status are all privileges and systems of advantages that we benefit from

Some of these are earned during life. White privilege is what people are naturally born with.

One subtle example of white privilege that children can understand easily is how plasters have always been designed for a lighter, white skin colour. So those with darker skin, black and brown people, have to use these 'skin-shade' plasters. It is only as recently as May 2020 following Black Lives Matter protests that the brand Band Aid has come up with a pack with multiple skin shades.

Another example is the box of crayons that children use. As a child, I remember drawing faces and colouring them with pink or peach-coloured crayons, confused because they looked nothing like me. There was either a dark brown colour or black in the set of crayons and pencil colours or pink and orange, none of which was like my own skin colour or that of those around me. Again, it was only recently in 2020 that the brand Crayola launched a 'colours of the world' pack that aims to represent the different skin colours from around the world, and that can help children see themselves in these colours. But the fact that it has taken until 2020 for something like this to be considered and designed is a sign of how whiteness is a norm, and white privilege pervades every aspect of our lives.

Acknowledging white privilege and understanding the role that it plays in systemic racism is not going to be enough to change the world. But this knowledge can give people the power to use it to support those who do not have this privilege.

> We need to be clear that there is no such thing as giving up one's privilege to be 'outside' the system. One is always in the system. The only question is whether one is part of the system in a way that challenges or strengthens the status quo. Privilege is not something I take and which I therefore have the option of not taking. It is something that society gives me, and unless I change the institutions which give it to me, they will continue to give it, and I will continue to have it, however noble and egalitarian my intentions.
>
> —HARRY BROD, 1989[9]

COLOUR BLINDNESS

I want my child to treat everyone the same. Children notice differences and have questions about them, but these are two very different things. Noticing difference but knowing that there is nothing to be ashamed of in it, or that difference is not the arbiter for equality, is important. Children have to be taught to appreciate and acknowledge differences and learn how to tackle these in a fair and judicious manner.

Some sociologists suggest that if we see colour it is

problematic as it can reinforce racist ideologies when one starts seeing oneself as member of a racial group. They have proposed that this can also reinforce white supremacy and white activism. However, a huge amount of research shows that as white people come to understand themselves as members of a racial group which has enjoyed unearned privileges and benefits, this can compel them to forge a different sense of white identity built on anti-racism rather than simply supporting the status quo. Moving away from the colour-blind ideology is actually an important step to acknowledging white privilege and towards anti-racist activism.

Colour blindness is silence around skin colour, saying that 'we do not notice skin colour'. Silence is also complicity in racism. It whitewashes the systemic racism in society and the history and legacy of oppression that people of colour carry, and it dismisses white privilege. Colour blindness encourages people to discount the systemic racism that affects the housing market, education and job opportunities, and it can lead to a dismissal of individual experiences of racism, particularly subversive microaggressions. Microaggressions are subtle acts of racism, such as making fun of someone's accent, excluding someone based on their different culture or ethnicity, dismissing someone's opinion because they are of a minority ethnic community, etc.

Children should know and understand that while it is OK to acknowledge skin colour, and that a person is 'black' or 'brown' or 'white', these labels should not be used to stereotype people and make generalised assumptions about a specific group. They have to be raised to be colour-conscious so that they acknowledge that skin colour has long been the basis for societal inequalities.

INTERSECTIONALITY

Intersectionality is an analytic framework for investigating categorical inequality. It maintains that looking at inequality linked to any one social division in isolation is misleading because multiple categories of social division (e.g. race, gender, sexuality, class, (dis)ability) intersect in ways that can exist together and are mutually reinforcing. Research on intersectionality is an understanding of power that is relational and contingent rather than fixed and binary.[10]

The term 'intersectionality' was coined in 1989 by Professor Kimberlé Crenshaw to describe how race, class, gender and other individual characteristics intersect with one another and overlap to create a more heightened form of bias or prejudice. According to African American Policy Forum (AAFP):

Intersectionality is a concept that enables us to recognize the fact that perceived group membership can make people vulnerable to various forms of bias, yet because we are simultaneously members of many groups, our complex identities can shape the specific way we each experience that bias. For example, men and women can often experience racism differently, just as women of different races can experience sexism differently, and so on.

Intersectionality can be sometimes viewed as a debate that becomes focused on labels rather than action. However, it is a useful word for understanding how different people can face more racial prejudice than others, even when they seem to belong to the same group. For children, this can help them understand that people have different experiences even when they are of the same race, and that none of these groups are monolithic. For example, often sexism and racism intersect so that black women might face more racial discrimination because they are both women and black. A person who is both gay and Latino would face a different set of prejudices than someone who is black and gay.

This means that as we try and help our children understand racism, we can also help them understand other forms of prejudice such as anti-Semitism, or prejudice against queer people of colour because of the way their identities intersect. And as they become aware of gender bias and disparities, they can understand better why women of colour might experience gender bias differently than white women.

WHITE-PASSING

Otherwise known as racial passing, white-passing happens when a person of colour belonging to a marginalised community 'passes' to identify as white. This term has become part of our social commentary and conversations as we realise that people who can pass as white hold a more privileged position amongst people of colour, because they also have a certain amount of white privilege due to the way they look. This shows how deep-seated white privilege is in our society. And this is also where an understanding of intersectionality can help. We have to consider the social hierarchies within minority ethnic groups. This dominance hierarchy is often designated on the basis of who can appear more 'white'.

The musician Halsey said on Twitter in June 2020[11] that:

> It would be an absolute disservice to claim that someone who is biracial but white-passing faces the same inequalities as other black people. I am in pain for my family, but nobody is gonna kill me based on my skin color.

The higher status and apparent desirability for light-skinned women of colour are well known in hip-hop lyrics and videos. Often women of colour on covers of prominent magazines and in media are the ones who have lighter skin, those who are seen to be more palatable to a white audience. Additionally, negative stereotypes rooted in colourism[12] are common in media representations of people of colour, with dark-skinned actors disproportionately cast as criminals compared with lighter-skinned actors. The lack of diversity on screen is startling, and even in Bollywood – India's primary film industry – only fair-skinned women get the leading roles. This creates a deep-rooted desire for lighter skin.

A research study by Texas Southern University[13] found that over a 15-year period it was lighter-skinned black women – the likes of Alicia Keys, Rihanna, Nicki Minaj, Mariah Carey and, of course, Beyoncé – who dominated Top 40 airplay in the pop charts. When Matthew Knowles, Beyoncé's father, was asked how different her career would have been had she been darker-skinned, he was unequivocal: 'I think it would've affected her success.' Beyoncé descends, via her mother's side, from Louisiana's 'Creoles of color' or *gens de couleur libres*', a distinct ethnic group that developed from unions between Europeans and Africans. They held a privileged position in society as compared with enslaved Africans; they were lighter-skinned and hence at the apex of the shade-based caste system, which still persists to this day.

With children of colour who are lighter-skinned and multiracial, this can be tricky to navigate as they often feel torn between their many identities. They can often lack the strong sense of belonging to their black or brown identity, as they do not look like others around them. On one hand, this affords them safety from racial abuse, yet it can also create a sense of confusion, shame or guilt. They may actively choose the predominant racial identity because it is easier and more comfortable to do so. Children who are white-passing may also feel that their identities and experiences can be dismissed when they are called 'almost white'.[14] No child should ever have to hide their true identity for the fear of discrimination and abuse.

Understanding the privilege that white-passing children have in our society is an opportunity to understand how even within brown and black communities there can be racial prejudice. Much of this is internalised racism, from the long history of colonialisation, which has fostered the belief that fair skin is superior. This is also the root of anti-blackness in South Asian communities. Proximity to whiteness can be seen as a goal. This means that people of colour can also be prejudiced against members of their own community.

If children understand the white privilege they carry because of being white-passing, they will learn to take responsibility and be better allies for the other members of the community who do not have the same advantages. And they can also stand up and speak up if their identities are policed, if their experiences are silenced, and if they are ever forced to choose one side of their identity over the other.

Why Am I Different?

Section II

Why Am I Different?

Children pick up messages about race and ethnic identity, and associated stereotypes and prejudices, from all around them. Here are some of the reference groups that enable and support a child's development of identity.

HOME

Parents, siblings and other extended family members are the first influence. These influences come from conversations, musical choices, the art that is around them, the food people eat, the books they read, the way they react to people around them, the TV shows they choose to watch, how they react to news. Children pick up on subtle cues at home and learn the biases and prejudices through words and actions of others.

SCHOOL

Teachers are another huge influence in a child's life, and as they grow older, their friends and peer groups grow important in how they define their identities. In looking at schools, we have to understand that the context shapes much of how children of different cultural backgrounds and ethnicities feel and learn. The dynamics and scale of racism and how it affects a child's racial identity and self-esteem will depend on the demographic of the school, of course. But more importantly it depends on how aware the school and the staff are of the value of racial education, and how deeply entrenched this is in their values and ethos. A child's perception of themself is shaped by how teachers react to particular human differences, and how instructional materials portray particular groups of people. Having a multicultural school with a large proportion of black and brown children does not necessarily mean that there will be less racism.

NEIGHBOURHOOD

The mix of people that live in your neighbourhood, the types of celebrations that are held and the resources available in the neighbourhood and local communities play a big part. Even though living in multicultural communities is great for introducing children to diversity, it does not automatically free children of racial biases, as they could easily be selectively picking up stereotypes. It is more important how integrated your community is.

FRIENDS

The way friends dress, the languages they speak and the holidays they celebrate open children's eyes to racial and ethnic differences. Friends become a very important reference group as children start school, and their own identities are often shaped by how they are perceived by their peer group.

MEDIA

Through TV shows, movies, music and the news, media is everywhere. It shapes understanding of race and ethnicity in its representations of the different groups in society. It can also create idealised standards of beauty based on skin and hair colour. Representation in media is a big issue.

Social media is a huge influence in children's lives these days through the people they follow, and the effect they have on their views and opinions. Young people want to be part of a community on social media and often this is driven by confirmation bias where they seek out views that are similar to their own, people who look like them, talk like them. This is probably not such a huge issue for children in the early years, but as they grow older, social media can reinforce stereotypes and assumptions and children can get caught up in echo chambers where their views are repeated back to them and they do not explore diverse views and representations. Social media is increasingly becoming a very significant reference frame for young people.

Social media can also be a mechanism for racial bullying that parents have to talk to their children about. Often children might think that sharing an offensive image or a joke via online platforms such as WhatsApp or TikTok is OK and not as harmful as real life. The online world can create the illusion of detachment from the real world. But children have to know that this is as offensive as face to face.

SOCIETY

The way systems such as education and the justice system treat the different groups in society plays a major role. This shapes a perception of social hierarchies as children find their own place in the world, especially concerning the respect that is afforded to different people based on their race or ethnicity.

These reference groups often intersect to shape a child's awareness and confidence in their racial identity, and how they view others who are different from them.

Section III

Birth to Three Years

Toddlers are continually forming a sense of familiar and unfamiliar objects and people, and through these forming a sense of their safety zone, and also their own identity. They start to develop a sense of race from the age of six months or so. Several studies conducted by the psychologists Phyllis Katz and Jennifer Kofkin found in 1997 that an infant is able to nonverbally categorise people by race and gender at six months of age, as they look for longer at an unfamiliar face from a different race than when they look at someone from their own race. Typically this is the time when children start to form a sense of separate self and this is the time when they start to associate a feeling of comfort or fear with certain people. But children are not born racists. They start assigning negative connotations to race as they grow older, which is why we need to start early.

The development of this self-concept is an important stage, where children are adding up their own personal identities plus that of the reference group, such as their family, to form a whole sense of themselves. This is what defines their sense of worthiness, a sense of who they are and where they fit in with the world.

For children of colour, or those with mixed racial

identities, the way that their reference group, their parents and educators see themselves, therefore, matters. This sense of security and of safety can come only when that group is feeling secure. This is why parents have to address their own racial traumas and experiences, and their own identities and biases as they bring up their children.

For white children, there can be an inherent sense transferred by social cues that whiteness is the standard, and that they are higher up in the social hierarchy. This is great for their own self-esteem because they see people like themselves everywhere, they don't have to doubt or question their own place in the world at a young age, but it can lead to a heightened sense of bias against those who do not look like them. It is also harmful because their sense of identity and self may be rooted primarily in their skin colour rather than in any other aspects of their personality.

Sometimes when parents have adopted children of a different race, or even children with a partner of a different race, there are a number of ingrained stereotypes that have to be overcome. In the book *The New Motherhoods*[15] there is an experience shared by a white European mother who had a child with an Asian partner. She talks about her preconceived assumptions that Asian children are quiet and obedient and sweet, and very musical or good at mathematics from a young age. And so such a parent would have to work really hard to question and unlearn these stereotypes when her child is born so as to help her child understand and acknowledge her Chinese heritage without being constrained by the stereotypes about her. Because if these internalised stereotypes are imposed upon her as expectations, this is internalised unconscious racism. The child will either feel limited and would have to conform to these in order to feel 'more Chinese', or else completely rebel against them and decline any associations with their Chinese heritage and identity.

Such internalised racism can also be expressed by extended family with statements such as 'I wonder how black the child will be'. Parents and family members may also feel a sense of loss when a child does not look exactly like them or like other children in the family because they are biracial. Sometimes this can cause undue scrutiny from strangers with doubts about whether the child is really yours. Recognition and acceptance from the parents and also from the extended family that the child does not look like them is a huge step in supporting the child to be comfortable with all aspects of their identity and not be torn by having to choose one 'side' or another.

In terms of identity development, young children are still at the 'pre-encounter' stage so they don't really see themselves as racial beings, do not understand why and how race matters, and do not have the language to describe their own racial identity or ideology. Children at such a young age are unable to process all the multiple dimensions associated with a person, and so they use 'transductive reasoning'. According to Jean Piaget, a developmental psychologist, children between the ages of two and four are unable to understand all the properties of social classes. Transductive reasoning is a faulty type of logic during this stage that involves making inferences from one specific to another. It is easier for them to look at someone's skin colour and use that to make generalisations about their other characteristics.

The pre-operational stage of cognitive development lasts from around two years old to seven years old, with the early pre-operational stage lasting from two to three years old. The key features of this stage include:

- Centrism: Children can often only think of one aspect of a situation at a time.
- Egocentrism: Children's view of the world is egocentric; they believe that other people see, hear and feel the same as them, and they can find it difficult to understand that people have different perspectives on the same situation.

This is also the age when their curiosity grows, and it is the time when children start to form a sense of stereotypes about how certain people act, assigning labels and generalised properties to groups of people. Facial cues are one of the primary determinants of these categorisations for young children, and so racial identity is beginning to deepen at this time.

Children will be observing and asking a lot of questions. They also try to explain the world around them, though this is largely egocentric (keeping themselves at the centre), and they explain any new occurrences based on their previous experiences and memories. So for instance a child who has been exposed to black men acting in a certain way will believe that all black men act in the same way.

This is the time when the cues that parents, educators and carers give out to the children matter a lot. But at this age they often lack the vocabulary to articulate their discomfort or curiosity around someone who looks different from them, so it might be expressed as fear or awkwardness. The notion of fear often stems from unfamiliarity and this can often be more the case with children who are growing up in monolithic environments (with predominantly one racial or cultural group) and do not encounter diversity and multiculturalism on a regular basis. Or they might stare openly, which can cause discomfort for the adults with them. Children are observing cues from parents and other caregivers. Do you hold them closer if you see a group of young men outside the supermarket, or do you get awkward when they point at someone and stare at someone? Children pick up on this discomfort, and this will influence how they perceive difference in the future.

Often parents can ignore, or pretend to ignore, questions and statements that pertain to difference, especially that concerning racial identities, because it is easier to do so. These statements and biases, if left unchecked and not questioned or actively countered, can lead to ingrained stereotypes and prejudices.

> My twins are the only children of colour at their preschool in the small town where we live, the staff are all white Europeans with local accents, and I am the only brown person they ever meet and see on a regular basis. It is a very white community and I am very conscious of how the twins would see and understand race. It is just around this age that my twins started forming a sense of familiarity and difference with the people around them. Their circle was becoming larger, and focus shifting from 'I' to 'them'. We visited India last year for the first time since they were born, and their initial reaction to people there was one of fear. This is not a permanent bias or prejudice at this stage, merely a fear of the novelty of someone who does not look like them. We sat next to an Asian-American family at Heathrow Airport on the way back

from India, and one of my twins could not stop staring at them. She was intrigued, and I could see that she was carefully observing me and her father, and our attitudes and behaviour towards this family, to take cues as to how she ought to feel about them. She wanted to get a sense of whether they were threatening or whether she could feel secure in their difference. This is where our nonverbal cues really mattered, the way we smiled and felt comfortable around them. As my otherwise socially reticent partner struck up a friendly conversation with this other family, within a few minutes our curious twins started to chat with the family and did not stop! It becomes our responsibility – as parents, teachers, educators – to teach our children racial socialisation, a strategy to understand race and racial difference, and of which societal messages to filter out and which ones to take on board.

Children start categorising and using power-based hierarchies in play based on the social cues they pick up from all the people around them, not just their parents. While thirty-month-olds show a preference for children of the same race when shown photographs of unfamiliar white and black children, demonstrating in-group bias, by the time they are thirty-six months old, the majority of children start choosing white play-mates. This study was carried out in the US,[16] where there are relatively homogeneous white communities. Context definitely matters, and so this pattern could be different in different cultural and social contexts. However, a similar study in Korea and India also indi-cated similar preferences, where white was considered better by the majority of children. This is highly likely to be a result of the implicit, as well as explicit, cues and messages these children receive from the people and media around them, where 'fair-skinned' is con-sidered more attractive. These instances can also lead to children internalising some of the biases they might encounter and starting to believe them, such as 'my hair is not blonde so I am not pretty, because only blonde hair is pretty'. This can result in poor social interactions and also low self-esteem.

Children are also very curious about physical charac-teristics of self and others, such as skin and hair colour. Children can be puzzled if all they see in toys and books is people and children who do not look like them. This is why diversity in books really matters. Children need to see themselves in these books, but they also need to see children of diverse backgrounds just doing 'normal' things, to show that despite our differences we can all be the same, and that skin colour alone cannot be a distinguishing feature. When parents or teachers are looking for diverse books for children, it is worth remembering that diversity is not enough. These books also have to actively question and shatter stereotypes and portray the children and people of colour in positive ways. While role models and representation matter for positive reinforcement and bolstering the self-esteem and identity of children of colour, or of mixed heritage, it is also extremely important that these are not reinforcing generalised assumptions of how certain people behave due to their skin colour.

With my two children being white-passing I am aware that they will enjoy the privilege that comes from proximity to whiteness. So there is always the tension of making sure that as I have any conversations about race with them, they do not feel forced to take any sides, they do not see their white father or relatives as villains, or even deny the Indian side of their heritage because it is more uncomfortable to accept and acknowledge it. I speak in Hindi as much as possible with them, and I have introduced them to Indian myths and stories. They are as comfortable calling their paternal grandmother 'Granny' as they are calling their maternal grandmother 'Nani'. We are also keen to make sure they travel and are exposed to different lifestyles and cultures. Going to India last year was eye-opening for them. Travelling also shows children that not everyone who has the same skin colour behaves in the same way, and it can make children aware of their own privileges and that people around the world live in different ways.

From a young age, as we read books, I started talking about people using comparisons such as what lovely dark hair they have, just like Mummy, or how lovely their green eyes are, just like Papa. This gives a cue to the child that people can have different colour skin and hair, and that is normal. We have talked about kindness and how a person seems to be helping others, or 'Oh that is a kind thing to do', to start introducing the concepts of compassion and a stepping stone to racial justice and equality at a later age.

Q 1: Why can't I be more like Papa?

When my child was around three years old, she started saying that she wanted to be just like her papa, and that she didn't like me at all. While it was upsetting, and I tried not to take it personally, there was an added dimension of whether she didn't want to be like me because in some way she considered my darker skin colour to be undesirable.

In the early years, we have to also weigh up normative developmental processes against any concerns about racial identity development. This is an important and often overlooked point. When my toddler expresses a desire to look just like her father, who is white, it is tricky to know whether she is merely developing an attachment bond by developing a strong identification with her father. A positive and deep bond with a parent is also an important step in developing a strong sense of self. Children go through phases and gravitate towards one parent or another at different times in their early years.

So in these early years, unless they have the whole language to articulate their racial identity and preferences, it is very difficult to know. At the same time, the reality of the race differences between parents can pose a complex and challenging task in supporting the child to integrate their own racial identity with that of either parent. Rather than ignoring it, or dismissing it as insignificant, we asked questions about why she wanted to be like her father. We looked at books about children with parents of different skin colours, and at books that showed diverse families, and we talked about the uniqueness of the child irrespective of how their parents looked. I remember lying back on the bed, with our forearms stretched out side by side and comparing our skin colours, and talking about how we were a rainbow family (rainbows were popular in our household at the time!). I think she wasn't as convinced of this as I was, but it started these very important conversations towards defining a strong identity. And these sparks are enough in these early years.

An honest and vulnerable piece in the *New York Times* parenting section by Norma Newton, a mother who is darker than her young child, offers a beautiful narrative of how children form a sense of beauty norms that create their biases and prejudices and so dark skin can become 'threatening' or 'ugly' for them. She writes how her mixed-heritage young child starts calling Newton's skin 'dirty' and expresses what many parents who have darker skin than their children, and who might have internalised the shame around their skin colour, must feel. We do not often hear stories like these publicly about the way that our mixed-heritage families form and develop a sense of self-esteem, tackling colourism and societal discomfort around darker hues of skin. Conversations matter.

Q 2: Why is she so brown?

I was in the local library when a small girl, probably around four years old, pointed at me and said loudly to her mother: 'Mummy, why is she so brown?' I could feel her mother getting very awkward and embarrassed, and she hastily shushed her, and moved away before I could say anything. This could be a key learning opportunity, where an age-appropriate conversation about people's uniqueness and differences could have been broached in a matter-of-fact way. Whenever my own children have asked about 'Why is that man in a wheelchair?' for instance, I have tried to talk about why some people might need wheelchairs, why sometimes our legs might not be able to carry our weight, and find stories and books about people in wheelchairs doing amazing things. We have then looked at biology books, and tried to talk about things we could do if we were in wheelchairs, and things we might not be able to do. In a similar vein, a conversation around difference in skin colour at this age could be approached with a response of 'Oh isn't it beautiful' or 'How wonderful that we are all so different and unique'. If an adult gets embarrassed about a question about brown skin, a child is likely to assume that there is something to be ashamed of or bad about having darker skin, especially if they do not see many people with dark skin around them.

Q 3: Why can't I have blonde hair? It is prettier.

One of my children came back from nursery one day and said that she wished she had blonde hair because 'it was prettier'. In that moment, I tried to reassure her that dark hair is very pretty, that she is also smart and clever and funny, and that is so very important. We also talked about how people are different, but they all look wonderful in their unique way. However, I heard her repeat this a few times again despite my assurances. Yes, there are no other children with dark hair and eyes like them at their nursery. And so most of the children they see around them are fair-skinned with blonde hair. These are also the images they see more regularly in the cartoons and films they are exposed to, despite our efforts to diversify media as much as possible. They've always seemed to have a sturdy belief in how wonderful and pretty they are. This was a red flag for me.

Here a few issues intersect, and while it is easier to dismiss this as a phase, and as an individual preference that a child should be allowed to explore, there is a power imbalance in how blonde hair is depicted and perceived in children's books, cartoons and toys as being better and superior. White, fair-skinned, blonde-haired, blue-eyed becomes the norm as children see this all around them. There is also plenty of research to show how linguistic categories, symbolism and labels give out implicit messages that 'whiteness' is good and positive, such as Snow White being 'white and pure', and negative things are associated with black, such as 'evil', 'dirty', 'wicked witch' and so on. This kind of 'smog'[17] that exists all around us creates an environment where children begin to apply these linguistic connotations to people.

Race has always been a contentious issue in how attractiveness is defined. Colourism remains a major issue in media – in print, television and films – in many

Asian and African societies. I remember reading parenting books when I was pregnant with P, and even in India the only books we could find were filled with these cute blonde babies. I am ashamed to admit now that I really wanted my child to be blonde and blue-eyed, even though I knew that it was genetically impossible. I am so deeply embarrassed about it, but it is internalised racialisation that I've had to unlearn over the years, and to break away from the notion of 'fair is lovely' that was so acutely ingrained in me from a young age.

Within Asian and African societies there is still a belief that the colour of a person's skin determines their worth and their attractiveness. This can be traced to India's centuries-old caste system, which is based on rigid hierarchies of social and hereditary occupations. The term for caste, *varna*, in India's ancient epic *Mahabharata* refers to skin colour. Here the Brahmins – the upper caste – were designated as white, while the lowest caste – the untouchables or the Dravidians – are described as dark or black; the darker your skin tone, the lower your place in the social hierarchy. Colour prejudice is widespread, and advertisements for products such as 'Fair & Lovely' face cream, the most popular skin-whitening cream, show dark skin as a barrier, and fair skin as a way to overcome the stigma of being born a girl and to achieve confidence and conquer 'womanly hesitation and fears'. Just looking at the matrimonial column in any Indian newspaper, or watching

Indian Matchmaking on Netflix recently, it is clear that skin colour is the constant and most important factor when finding a prospective partner. This has also perpetuated and enabled anti-black sentiment in Asian communities.

The data-analysis company The Pudding looked at 19 years of *Vogue* magazine covers, spanning 228 issues with a total of 262 female cover models, using a combination of facial recognition and clustering techniques to blur the background, pixelate the faces, and then identify which of the pixels were showing 'skin'. They used a scale of 'lightness' as a standard measure to compare all the models across the 228 issues. The results were startling but hardly surprising: until 2015 no solo black model had featured on the cover of *Vogue*, over a span of 146 issues, since Naomi Campbell in 2002. At the beginning of the research in 2000, even the models on the darker shade of the spectrum had very light skin, such as Halle Berry. Sometimes, as in the case of Lupita Nyong'o on the cover of *Vanity Fair*, photographs of black models have been digitally manipulated to make them look lighter, to create the impression of a white-passing woman of colour, a phenomenon called 'whitewashing'. As children are growing up, this Western, Eurocentric standard of beauty can create internalised self-loathing. Children begin to get the message that striving for beauty isn't just a matter of presenting our best self, but of fundamentally changing their self with things like hair-straightening chemicals and toxic skin-lightening creams. Lupita Nyong'o talked about feeling this impact, saying: 'I remember a time when I, too, felt unbeautiful. I put on the TV and only saw pale skin. I got teased and taunted about my night-shaded skin. And my own prayer to God, the miracle worker, was that I would wake up lighter-skinned.'

Black women have for centuries been forced to conform by straightening their hair. This tide is turning with celebrities like Michelle Obama and Lupita Nyong'o leading the way, and Maria Borges being the first ever Victoria's Secret model to wear natural black hair.

Hlonipha Mokoena, associate professor at the Wits Institute for Social and Economic Research, University of the Witwatersrand, writes in an article that one of the first insults she remembers from school is someone telling her 'your hair feels like pubic hair'. Black hair has been considered unruly, wild, and also policed to suit the white gaze and sensibilities. There was also a sort of law called 'Tignon Law'[18] in Louisiana in the 1800s as a part of what was called the *Bando du buen gobierno* (Edict for Good Government) which demanded that all women of colour cover their hair with a cloth. What these rules were meant to do was try to curtail the growing influence of the free black population and keep the social order of the time. The law was based on the belief that the overly ostentatious hairstyles of black women drew the attention of white men and the jealousy of white women, and made both white men and women feel uncomfortable. In slave societies, white women would often hack off the hair of their enslaved female servants.

If your child has blonde hair and lighter skin, then it is also important to remind them that it is not the only way to be beautiful, to dismantle the ideas around white supremacy. It is also crucial to reaffirm the idea that beauty is more than skin-deep, and that hair or skin colour is not a determinant of beauty, and that in different cultures and contexts historical beauty standards change. Many parents have shared their experiences of this with me:

> My husband has Jamaican heritage and our daughter is very white and has blonde ringlets and blue eyes. People constantly remark on how strange and wonderful this is in a way my husband (quite fairly) finds offensive.
>
> 'She is so lucky to have blonde hair.'
> 'Oh, she is so gorgeous with blonde hair and blue eyes. Shame that her sister didn't get these genes.'

These are stereotypical properties associated with skin and hair colour, and even as I tweeted about this a number of women told me that 'blondes have more fun'. We need to be aware of comments that elevate the status of fair-featured or blonde-haired children by showing positive biases towards them or negative biases towards others. These comments can come from strangers or family members, but they are the social cues that start to influence children's racial identities and self-worth from a young age.

Many parents of colour have shared their own experience of growing up and feeling rejected because they could not be cast as an angel in school plays because 'angels always have blonde hair'. I was also reminded of the time when P was eight or nine and part of a small theatre group where she was made to wear a blonde wig to play a princess in their performance. It was profoundly saddening to see it being reinforced at such a young age that the princesses needed to have blonde hair.

When young children say these things – either wishing that their own skin or hair colour was different or prettier, or believing that they are beautiful because they have certain traits – it is based on the messages that they hear around them that certain physical traits are superior. While dismantling these ideas, we also have to give their feelings space, and find out more about why they think so.

One of our conversations recently went something like this:

'Why do you think blonde hair is prettier?'

'Because it is. It looks beautiful.'

'But I have dark hair and I think I am very pretty. I think you are smart and clever and funny, and you are very beautiful.'

'But Elsa has blonde hair. And all my friends have blonde hair.'

'But remember Frida Kahlo[19] had dark hair. And she was amazing, wasn't she? And you are so unique for having hair that is different from others, aren't you?'

One of the books that they have really loved is *The Crayon Box that Talked*, and so I realised that I could use it to explain difference to them. We talked about how each crayon was unique and how each had something special to offer when they make a drawing, and how boring it would be if all the crayons were the same colour, or if they just had one crayon in the box. This was something that was really simple and effective.

And then after a couple of days, we looked at some pictures of women and men with dark hair. We talked about how we have darker hair because my mother and father had dark hair, and because she is very unique with Indian heritage. And we looked at some books on Indian mythology and history to remind her of the amazing men and women who were strong, clever and smart and did not have blonde hair. We stood side by side in front of the mirror, and made silly faces, and brushed our hair together, and talked about how much we looked like each other, and how wonderful that was.

Other parents have taken different approaches to this.

'A few years ago my daughter said something similar, so we've had lots of chats, I deliberately dyed my hair darker and bought books that promoted strong/ brave/smart girls. She now loves her brunette locks and wants to be a scientist – here's hoping!'

Once again, parents cannot do this work alone, so if your child is at preschool or nursery, it is important to initiate a conversation with the teachers about what they are doing to bring in diversity and racial equality in the classroom, to assess what physical artefacts such as toys and books they have, the dress-up clothes that can all contribute to this notion of idealised beauty and to racial stereotypes.

In growing up in a culture that devalues black skin or hair, or shows a preference for a fair skin and blonde hair, many children of colour grow up denying or disliking a crucial part of themselves. And white children can grow up with an internalised sense of superiority or a perception that they are the norm. This has to be, therefore, addressed from a very young age.

CHECKLIST

◆ Understand that your own upbringing will affect your parenting.

◆ Unlearn your own biases and prejudices.

◆ Reflect on your racial trauma and experiences.

◆ Be mindful of your own words and actions.

◆ Make it OK to ask questions from a very young age.

◆ Introduce diverse books and question stereotypes.

◆ Be picky with literature and media they are exposed to.

◆ Make sure children see themselves in the books.

◆ Introduce positive stereotypes and role models.

◆ Foster pride in children's racial identity.

◆ Introduce stories of your own culture and heritage.

◆ Use the right terms and vocabulary.

◆ Introduce critical thinking (true/not true, fair/ not fair) about stereotypes and situations they see in books and cartoons.

◆ Widen your own circle of friends and acquaintances.

- ◆ Travel, if possible, to expose children to different lifestyles and cultures.
- ◆ Collaborate with teachers and educators to promote learning about each other's home cultures and each other's similarities and differences.

Four to Six Years

Section IV

Four to Six Years

As children enter school years, this is the time when the acknowledgement of similarities and differences extends to an awareness that these have the power to exclude and include people in peer groups and friendships. Besides their families, children now also want to feel a sense of belonging with their friends and peer groups. Beyond just noticing similarities and differences, they are also noticing attitudes associated with their own skin colour, and they will start feeling excluded or included amongst their peer groups. This is really the time when children start comparing themselves to others and forming a sense of whether they belong or not. This 'fitting in' starts becoming more important to them. Any exclusion could also be because of accent, size, religion and so on. These categories will intersect with race and can heighten the bias that children of colour encounter, especially if they are in the minority in their school.

Children are becoming more sociocentric rather than egocentric as in the earlier years of their life. As they are growing out of their early *pre-operational stage* and the egocentrism is diminishing, they can be engaged in 'let's pretend' and role play which can be very useful with discussion scenarios and concepts related to racism. Many children can also start to understand that different people may have different views on things. They have a more sophisticated model of the world around them than what Jean Piaget, the Swiss psychologist, gave them credit for in his model of cognitive development.

Their sense of individual identity evolves into group identity both cognitively and emotionally and they start becoming conscious of being part of a group different from other groups. They want to know more about their own group and start developing a sense of pride in their group. This in itself is not the basis of bias or prejudice, but their sense of any discrimination against their group is also heightened, which can lead to a strong in-group/out-group bias. Children are also forming their identities and sense of place and belonging through formation of in-groups and out-groups.

During these years, if the child sees a mismatch amongst their different reference groups, between their family, school and friends and how they treat them, and also between each other, they can start hiding parts of their identities so as to try and fit in. This is why it is important to start working on a child's self-esteem at preschool age, so that they are self-confident but also have a healthy curiosity, are open-minded and accepting of others. Now is the time for parents to start talking more openly about identities, and helping children navigate their identities in a non-judgemental and safe space so that they don't feel the pressure to conform.

Research has shown that both black and white children are more likely to choose white dolls than black dolls. Choosing fair-skinned dolls over dark-skinned dolls may be an early sign of the child rejecting their own identity in favour of a whiter one, and this sign should be addressed as soon as it starts coming up. If children are taking this approach to forming their own identity, they may reject those who look like themselves, and they may feel like an outsider in their own families and communities as they grow older. They start internalising the message that whiteness is the norm, and that there is something to be ashamed of about their own culture and heritage, or even their skin colour. This means that they can start imitating other groups, which may not let them in, because they are seen as outsiders. This can isolate them from all the groups, and that can be a lonely place to be in.

Research has shown that children at this age create assumptions related not only to skin colour but also to lifestyle, language and religious belief. Name-calling in general, and racist name-calling in particular, has been shown to be an important tool used by some children in the assertion of their status with one another. They start becoming more sensitive to their environment and surroundings and how they fit in or feel excluded.

Benjamin Brooks-Dutton, author and entrepreneur, who has a nine-year-old dual-heritage son, shared this with me:

'I first noticed how socially conscious he was at around the age of five or six. He'd often ask if he would be the only black or dual-heritage child at a party or gathering, and if I said "yes" he often wouldn't want to go.'

This is the time to start modelling positive actions along with the groundwork that you have laid out in the early years. This is also the time when you need to start making sure that children value and take pride in their own cultural heritage, because the pressure from outside will be greater than ever, competing for a child's attention. You should also start focusing on language and words, even though we are often too exhausted to check for everything our child is picking up from friends and peers in the classroom and playground. Children often pick up these words from media and parents, and they can carelessly throw words around that reinforce stereotypes around race.

A black parent shared with me that even though they have tried very hard to disrupt any racial stereotypes at home, their six-year-old son has suddenly started saying things such as 'Black men are much tougher than white men' or 'Black men are stronger'. An engaged honest conversation about how and why they picked up this stereotype really matters. This can be a way for a child to navigate their identity and to help them feel more empowered if they are feeling left out at school, or if they have been made to feel inferior by their peers. It is important to try and step into the child's shoes and see the world from their eyes where possible. Children might be asking more questions around differences now and ascribing value judgements to these, such as 'All black children have crazy hair' or 'All brown people eat curry'. As parents, it is easy to laugh at these or ignore them, but what you need to do is to listen for any value judgements kids may be unknowingly placing on those differences, such as skin colour or hair texture, and then gently correct them. Just saying 'Don't say that' or ignoring it is not enough. It is important to challenge any prejudice. As parents we have to seize teachable moments when we can. Asking non-judgemental questions such as 'Why do you think like that?' or 'What makes you say this?' will help you understand where that assumption comes from, and why the child is making it. This means that you have more information on why these stereotypes were formed, and can work with the child in addressing them and explaining why most stereotypes are not true.

Children at this age are still learning how to put their feelings into words, and can resort to reductive statements where they easily fall back into the misguided idea that in order to be black, for instance, they have to conform to some set of characteristics, such as speaking or acting in a certain way. So while a child understands and takes pride in their ethnicity and heritage, it is important they understand that while others may treat them in a specific way because of their skin colour or label assigned to them, they are not defined by this label.

If a white child expresses such sentiments about black men as above, it is crucial and urgent to discuss why they think like this, and to disrupt this negative stereotype as quickly as possible. Research has shown that black men are more associated with aggressiveness and criminality, and such harmful stereotypes can lead to, for instance, more police brutality and incarceration for black men even when they have not committed a crime. A child has to understand that how a person looks on the outside is less important than how they act towards other people. We cannot judge people on how they appear. This is also an important moment to discuss how black men might experience more racism because of such stereotypes.

We need to help children see beyond labels such as 'black' and 'white', which can mean that they lump everyone they identify as such into one homogeneous mass, and create a generalised assumption about them. At this age, they can also still associate group memberships with certain specific actions or attributes:

'I cannot be Indian because I do not like Indian food.'

'Chinese people are good at maths.'

'Mexican people always take the bus.'

'Black men are very strong.'

Once they start putting people into categories and assigning labels and value judgements, slowly and steadily they can start forming biases and prejudices against a group that they do not see as their reference group, those who are part of the out-group, those whom they do not identify with, those who do not look like them.

Some children are more sensitive than others. I know one of my four-year-old twins worries, and is prone to anxiety. She lies there for hours at night worrying about everything that could happen to her or to us. And she needs a lot of reassurance. I have to broach any topics cautiously with her, in a very matter-of-fact way without bringing emotion into it. This can be tricky, as talking about racism can be fraught with emotion. But with most children at this age you have to focus on facts, in as simple language as possible, in the most matter-of-fact manner. Recently she saw a newspaper image of a policeman arresting someone, and asked me: 'Will the police come and get me too?' I was taken aback, and initially I wanted to sweep it away, just allay her fears, and make sure her childhood innocence wasn't shattered. But it gave me an opportunity for a teachable moment. I chatted with her about some police officers treating some people differently because of their skin colour because they might believe that everyone who is black is more 'bad' than 'good'. But they might see brown people differently. And we want to be careful, cautious and aware, but not all police officers would judge people based on their skin colour. I gave her positive examples of what people in law enforcement do, how they help others, and why that is so important.

If I am honest, I did feel uncomfortable, but I want to parent as an ally, and so I have to teach my child that the police and other people in power and other people we trust, much like anyone else, can be biased and treat people differently because of their skin colour. But this is not how everyone is, and we can change things. We talked at some length about why we should never judge anyone based on how they look. And then we went and bought some ice creams so that she could remember a positive moment at the end of this conversation.

Many parents wait for their children to mention race, and assume that if they have not brought up anything then it is not an issue. But research has shown that children are thinking about differences even if they do not talk about them explicitly. The age between four and six years old is crucial because children are inquisitive about the world, but still not able to reason rationally about why people who look different are not different from one another.

As a woman of colour, who came to this country as a young single parent to study for a PhD, working in predominantly white spaces, I thought that talking about race would make it more visible. I thought that if I didn't mention my race, or talk about it explicitly with my daughter, it would not be an issue. I didn't want to draw attention to my race so as to not feel that I had been given any opportunity because of positive discrimination or tokenistic diversity. But I was completely wrong. Because no matter what, skin colour is the first thing a person notices about another. In not talking about race, I did not prepare my eldest daughter adequately for any racial bullying she faced, and she felt disconnected from her own heritage – trying to disclaim her Indianness, refusing to speak Hindi or to dress up in Indian clothes outside home. Even though we talked a lot about standing up and speaking for ourselves, empowering her with regular debates and discussions, role models in books and media, and

> modelling such behaviour myself, I
> focused this primarily on gender rather
> than race. It was perhaps because I myself
> grew up in India where I experienced
> gender bias but not racial bias.

It is natural that a parent's own experience would shape how they bring up their children, either because they have been brought up in a colour-blind manner and believe that it is the best approach or because they have faced racial abuse and trauma themselves and find it extremely triggering to talk about race. Sometimes immigrant parents do not discuss racism with their children, instead preparing them to 'fit in' and 'not create a fuss'. But this can create a huge crisis of identity, and fails to get the children ready to face the realities of the world around them.

History is always a good vehicle for teaching about racism. Some parents and teachers shared with me that they had been looking at the civil rights movement in the United States to help children understand oppression against black people. One parent shared:

'Black people were not allowed access to some things a long time ago. We know better now.'

The intention is honourable but the problem is that this creates the misconception that racism is a thing of the past. It is not. Children need to understand and acknowledge this.

Sometimes history has to be made personal and linked to family stories for the child to understand why it matters. For instance, when Benjamin first started talking about the transatlantic slave trade with his son, he found it tricky to engage fully with what seemed to him an abstract concept, and something that happened a long time ago.

'He had Jamaican grandparents and so he needs to know about it, because without it he arguably wouldn't exist. However, there's little point me trying to explain how millions of enslaved people from African countries died as a result of this genocidal period of history, because he can't picture millions of people. Instead, I ask him to try to picture his grandparents' ancestors and then think about his name and how that was passed to us by slavers. It makes it real for him and helps him understand that it's so personal that it can't simply be dismissed as another lesson he doesn't want to learn.'

It is through history that we know and understand our own and others' place in the world. It is important for our children to hear our stories, and that of their ancestors. We should talk about their history so that they take pride in their roots, and don't reject their racial and cultural heritage. This way they can understand their place in the world, and also learn to express their own heritage. Bi-racial children, in particular, can sometimes be forced to choose one part of their heritage over another. Discussing intergenerational narratives and history will lead to a stronger sense of identity. Stories of their grandparents and parents shared across the dinner table have been shown to shape children's personal narratives, and result in a deeper sense of rootedness and well-being. These connections across generations help children find a sense of self. Research has shown that children who grow up in an open environment at home, with honest and open conversations around racism, and hearing family stories are more likely to develop critical thinking around their own identities and those of others around them.

The history that British schoolchildren are taught is a sugar-coated, whitewashed version which focuses on the 'good bits': wars fought and won, and the white men who were victorious. Children have to understand who writes history, and whose history it is. Any black history that is taught in schools in the UK is mainly from the African American perspective, and children often only know about Martin Luther King and Rosa Parks. On the other hand, a quick review of the school curriculum shows a distinct lack of information about British colonialism, the imperial rule and its impact on the colonies, and Britain's role in slave trade. Ever as they study the world wars, the various African and Indian soldiers who fought side by side with the English soldiers are completely ignored in this narrative. Thus white children see a very white-centric view of British history, where the minority ethnic communities are completely invisible. And brown and black children continue to see themselves as outsiders, with the history of their ancestors not intertwined with the nation's history. While we do this work of not only reading these texts but also supporting our children in interpreting what they see, hear and read, we have to remember to interpret much of the knowledge in the context in which it was produced.

> With my own children, I have talked
> about how our family was affected by
> the colonial rule in India. While one of
> their maternal great-grandparents lost
> everything, his farm and livelihood, which
> completely changed their lives, their
> other great-grandfather worked for the
> British and reached a senior position
> (as high as Indians were allowed within
> the hierarchy, where they were lower
> than the British) in the government.
> This discussion raised interesting points
> about the effect of oppression, and
> also the notion of privilege, and how we

benefit from the privilege that we inherit through our ancestors. It was also useful to discuss that within systemic racism there is always a sense of being grateful for what we can get, which can create a sense of internalised racism, but also prejudice against other members of our own community. Narrating our family story was a useful stepping-stone to understanding imperialism, its legacy, and how anti-blackness seeps into the South Asian community, where the centuries of internalised racial hierarchy resulted in the belief that fair-skin is superior.

While you talk about history of colonialism and slavery with your children, make sure to emphasise that there were always allies, those who stood side by side with the oppressed irrespective of their race. And it is important to talk about this in terms of some people acting in an unfair way, rather than people of a certain skin colour always being bad or good. It is easy for children to transfer these properties to the whole group, and assign value judgements in the present as they learn about the past.

Continuing to diversify children's books and reading is of course still very important. But it is even more crucial that any role models and representation they encounter in their books do not perpetuate a specific view of a community. Sometimes books written by white people about other cultural groups can reinforce stereotypes. Or these books, even when they feature people of colour, may tackle the subject very superficially and in a colour-blind manner. For instance, many of the books for young children about Rosa Parks or Martin Luther King offer no real background or understanding of the social and historical context of the slave trade and segregation. Eminé Rushton, editor of *Oh* magazine, says that after reading a book about Rosa Parks, a story with a happy ending that somehow gives the impression that the world was now a fair, happy and loving place because of Rosa, her daughter was very confused about why racism still exists. Definitely use these books, but deploy them as mediators for a deeper and more explicit discussion.

To counter white supremacy we also have to read and support writers of colour. But often such books used in schools are from writers who write about being the minority, about race and of being othered. While it is very important for children to understand the experience of those who may be different from themselves, this creates a singular narrative in which the diversity within these communities is not shown. Often, some of the texts that are chosen at school are quite simple in structure and content with an assumption that students will find diverse views and settings challenging. Much of the teaching in classrooms, even when part of a diversity initiative, is well-meaning but often incredibly simplistic. This is usually the case when teachers are uncomfortable with discussing race, and haven't had an opportunity to reflect on and unlearn their own unconscious biases. And so they remain at a comfortable and superficial level. This perpetuates a colour-blind approach which has to be questioned and countered at home, meaning that parents have to work harder to introduce books that do the opposite.

It is important to bring in writers who write about varied things. In media, movies and books there are bodies and voices that are not actively represented. Parents can actively challenge and question these representations and discuss with children what is missing or how a representation might be missing certain viewpoints, and why certain groups are often represented in stereotypical ways. One way of doing this, while ensuring that a child remains actively engaged in choosing their own books, is to help them in curating their reading by suggesting that from every three books they choose in the library or in a bookshop, at least one always has to be written by a writer of colour, or with people of colour as the main protagonists. This ensures that children read around their own interests but also diversify their reading, and start taking responsibility for tackling systemic racism.

Children's exposure to diversity should not just be limited to the school day or to the neighbourhood they live in. A parent with two children aged four and six shared this in one of the anti-racism workshops I ran:

'We live in a town which is very white. Most of the children in my daughter's class at school are white, except I think three children who are brown-skinned. We have lots of books with diverse characters but in our everyday life the people around my children are predominantly white. I am worried that they are growing up without seeing diverse people and experiences.'

Parents can be deliberate about the activities they get their children involved in outside school, and they can find clubs and groups where they will be exposed to more diversity. Children are not too young to get involved in volunteering too, where they may encounter people from different backgrounds. This can also prompt discussions about how their privileges in terms of race, class and gender might afford them certain benefits in society that others do not share.

A white parent of a six-year-old shared this with me after he attended one of my workshops for parents:

'We went to a protest and my child asked me what we were protesting about. I explained to them that police had killed a black man. Suddenly he asked me "Are black people not safe?" I said "No, because some people still think that anyone who is black is bad." He understood that this is wrong. We had a conversation about how black people might be treated differently to white people. He understood that he is safer because he is white, and that it is not fair that some people are treated differently than others.'

And right there was a discussion about white privilege without even mentioning the term.

As children start school, it is important for you to monitor what practices and things such as books, toys and images they are encountering there. I have faced a lot of resistance and often tokenism from teachers and schools when I have tried to bring up issues of diversity and racial education, because often stepping outside the normal curriculum takes time and effort, and teachers have to unlearn their own biases as well. But do not be afraid to ask questions. When schools do not actively – and aggressively – try to facilitate positive identities for all their students, including their racial identity there are consequences. Extensive research has shown that children from minority ethnic backgrounds suffer stereotypes and low expectations from teachers as soon as they start primary school. They are also more likely to be punished and suspended for minor infringement that may be ignored in other students. This can shape a child's expectations of themselves and a limited view of their potential. This can also expose them to stereotype threat at a young age, where they are anxious and stressed because they are hyper-aware of being stereotyped. We know that achievement success is mediated both by belief in one's capability and by the quality of school experiences and social interactions. Children need to be immersed in a school environment which values racial identity, and does not take a colour-blind approach to education. There has to be an open dialogue between teachers and parents. Parents cannot do this work alone once children start school.

One very useful activity at this age is to talk actively about how a child sees themself. Ask them to describe themselves and get them to draw themselves. What kind of words do they use for self-identification? Self-portraits are a good insight into how a child's identity is being shaped. Children are forming a sense of themselves and their world as pieces of jigsaw puzzle. Rather than focusing on their artistic skills, which can vary from child to child, self-descriptions and portraits will show which pieces of their own puzzle they have figured out. If a black child colours herself with a pink or peach crayon or makes her hair straight, it might show that they are creating an identity based on what they want to look like, what they think is more desirable and the societal norm, rather than what they actually look like. And this is where an intervention and discussion is needed to help them be more confident in themselves and their own unique identity.

Q 4: Why are people's skin colours different?

This is a great opportunity to talk about melanin in skin, and how skin serves the same purpose no matter what its colour is. It has a protective purpose. It is relatively straightforward to say that people who have more melanin will have darker skin. It is also easy to say that children come in different shapes, sizes and appearances, including different skin colours, and this is what makes us all unique. When my eldest, P, was around five years old, she refused to drink chocolate milk because she thought that it would make her skin browner and darker. We had a conversation about melanin, and we also looked at biology books that show the structure of skin, and what it does. And we considered why darker skin might be useful and better for her. We looked at some photographs online of beautiful men and women with darker skin, which inspired a lot of pride in her about her skin colour.

One parent asked me:

'My child is confused how children with dark brown skin can be African-American, Indian or Hispanic. I am not sure how to explain this to them.'

Here, once again, remind them that skin colours lie on a spectrum and that labels assigned by society do not define people. People can form identities based on nationality or cultural origin. So while we teach our children that skin colour does not have any biological significance in terms of its connection to intelligence, beauty, or criminality or aggressiveness, we have to, at the same time, make them aware that it has cultural and historical significance.

Q 5: If my friend is black then why isn't his mum black?

Skin colour is determined by melanin, the pigment responsible for dark skin in humans.[20] Groups of people whose ancestors lived closer to the equator – where there's more ultra-violet radiation – tend to have darker skin.[21] What skin colour we have is determined by the combination of our genes and how they get mixed up.

Many genes influence the production of melanin, as well as environmental factors such as sunlight. The genes that control the amount of melanin in someone's skin operate under 'incomplete dominance', meaning that neither the gene for lighter skin nor that for darker skin can gain prominence over the other. Visually this will mean a mixed-race child's skin tone will be a mix of its parents, lying anywhere on the spectrum between the two.

Your child's friend might appear more 'black' and have darker skin colour than their mother who is 'white' or other ethnicity with lighter skin colour. But self-identification is important. If their friend has darker skin colour, that does not automatically mean that they are 'black'. They could be South Asian, or Hispanic, or Mediterranean. It is important not to assume automatically that a person identifies as black. You can explain to your child that even if the mother does not appear black, she might be 'mixed-race', which means that she might be more fair-skinned than other black people. This does not mean that she does not identify as black. Or, even if she is white, it is possible that the child has inherited more of the genes that determine a darker skin colour, from the father, or one of their ancestors.

No person is 100 per cent white-skinned or 100 per cent dark-skinned. They are always a mix of different tones, and whichever is more dominant becomes more visually prominent. But society tends to fall back on rigid labels so that people are often labelled black or white depending on which end of the spectrum their skin colour lies closer to.

People often assume that a child and parent, especially a mother, would always have the same skin colour. With my own white-passing mixed-race children, I have sometimes been confused for their nanny, due to my darker skin. Discussing biology and genetics with children in an age-appropriate manner can help them understand how skin colour is inherited, and how identities are shaped due to cultural heritage but also based on how society perceives a certain person.

Q 6: Should I make friends with children who don't look like me?

No, not *just* because they look different, though it is important we give everyone a chance. It is important that children make a real effort to understand differences, and be curious about different cultures and experiences. Being friends with diverse people can help them realise that while labels matter in how people are treated, they don't define the person. Children who have diverse friendship groups will be more open-minded to new experiences and people as they grow older, less likely to carry stereotypes and biases, and more likely to stand up against racial injustice.

It is important that we teach our children to try and make as diverse friendship groups as possible. Children might reject or exclude those who do not look like them, especially if they notice these attitudes at home, or if you do not have very diverse friendship circles. If they haven't been exposed to diverse representation in books and media before they start school, they might carry some stereotypes that are based on the fear of the unfamiliar. These stereotypes can become deeply ingrained and then it can become too late to overturn some of their biases. Yes, children should choose friends based on who they like and who they want to spend time with. On the other hand, we all know that confirmation bias can create echo chambers. If you think about it, you are more likely to spend time with those who look like you, act like you, think like you, in real life and especially on social media. This means that your views are being echoed back at you and you are likely to stay in this comfort bubble. You should encourage these diverse friendships, rather than force them. Perhaps one way would be to arrange play dates with children from different racial and ethnic backgrounds.

However, it is worth remembering that just because your child plays and is friends with children of different races, it does not mean that you can adopt a colour-blind approach to raising them. It does not mean that they do not notice skin colour. It does not mean that they will not carry any racial bias. Even though diverse friendship groups should be encouraged, and children are given the message of 'do not judge a book by its cover', you still have to do the work and talk to them actively about race and racism.

Q 7: Why am I being treated differently?

How do we prepare our children against discrimination? This cannot just be a one-off conversation. All children can benefit from talking openly about diversity and bias. But for kids in groups more likely to be a target of discrimination, such conversations can be even more critical.

We know from research conducted by the American Association of Pediatrics that experiencing racial discrimination or even seeing racial discrimination can have a huge mental and physical impact on a child's health. Children can also be affected by any injustice they see around them. Perceived discrimination has been linked to physical and mental health problems including anxiety, depression, obesity, high blood pressure and substance abuse. Many of these problems are believed to stem from the chronic stress associated with being a potential target of discrimination. Anxiety leads to the release of the stress hormone cortisol, which can lead to chronic health conditions. Discrimination-related stress can also affect how kids feel about themselves. It might prevent them from speaking up in class, or from participating in activities that are important to them.

Racial bullying in classrooms and playgrounds can take various forms, such as being treated differently or excluded because of skin colour, name-calling or jokes about skin colour, nationality or culture.

'You cannot play with us because you wear a turban.'

'You smell of curry.'

'Why do you have such weird hair?'

Several parents, for instance, have mentioned to me that their black or dual-heritage children have their hair touched a lot even by strangers. 'Mixedness' can often be fetishised, which is also a form of racial discrimination and prejudice. Children should be equipped to know how to handle it if strangers ask to touch their hair, or touch it without their permission. Children have to be taught boundaries around their own bodies, and learn to say that it is not OK for others to comment on their skin colour or their hair. They should, in turn, also learn that it is not OK to go and touch a child's hair or call it 'crazy' or 'weird'.

So it is important to talk to children and empower them in knowing how to deal with an unfairness associated with their own skin colour. Talking openly with children can prepare them for dealing with discrimination and help them keep discrimination-related stress in check. If you have been talking about race and discrimination for a while, then this can be an ongoing conversation and children will already have some understanding of why they are being perceived as different. Children can be prepared to recognise signs of racism, and to have some prepared comeback remarks. Teach young people how to speak up about disrespectful language directed at themselves or others, and set boundaries, by saying things such as:

'That didn't sound kind.'

'That sounds prejudiced.'

'Please stop saying that.'

'Please move out of my way.'

Here role play can help children prepare reactions to any situation where they feel threatened or excluded. Also be clear that you will understand if they don't feel safe speaking up. In such situations, they should feel OK to get adult help. At this age, while it is important they learn to stand up for themselves where they feel comfortable to do so, they should not be dealing with such situations on their own, and they should feel empowered to ask for help, even from busy adults. Asking for help and support is not a sign of weakness. Asking for help in a clear manner is important with words such as: *'Please listen to me. This is important.'*

Give them tools so that they can bounce these harmful or insulting things back and understand that they do not have to internalise any racism they encounter. The 'dustbin' technique can help children actively refuse to accept any insults hurled at them. For example, if someone says to them 'I don't want to sit with you' or 'I don't want to be your friend', they can metaphorically throw these words away rather than absorbing and internalising them, by saying 'I will find someone else to sit with' or 'I will find another friend'. If a child has been supported in developing a strong identity and self-worth, they can be taught to tackle exclusion with resilience.

Depending on the level of discrimination or bullying a child has faced, the school should be involved in this too. School governors and school boards have to be mindful of the laws that cover racial discrimination and bullying. If a child has felt excluded, then their feelings are valid. Saying 'I am sure they didn't mean it' is not the right approach. Instead, help children find the language to articulate how they are feeling. Give them space for their feelings, even if our natural urge is to jump in and reassure them or distract them from feeling uncomfortable or unhappy.

When you talk about history with your children, it is important to talk about the activism within these communities who faced such oppression, and the resilience and strength that people showed. Doing so helps children understand that people can always stand up and speak up. This can empower children so that they do not see themselves or others from their heritage as victims. For instance, Viola Desmond, a black woman, challenged racial segregation in Nova Scotia in 1946 and was later the first Canadian woman to be featured on a $10 bill. Desmond's story can show children the idea that people can make a change based on their actions. This can show them that if they ever face racism they have the choice to resist.

Finally, if you've had conversations with your child about how people can treat others differently because of their skin colour or other differences, then they will be better prepared to recognise it, and deal with it when it happens to them. They will know that any exclusion has less to do with them, and more with the stereotypes and prejudices that others hold.

CHECKLIST

- ◆ Maintain diversity in toys and books.
- ◆ Decolonise the curriculum and education.
- ◆ Question and actively challenge negative views and stereotypes children see in movies, cartoons, books.
- ◆ Ask teachers questions about what books children are reading, and what the school's racial education framework and policy is.

- Be mindful of your own implicit and overt actions and words.
- Actively challenge prejudiced views and statements rather than ignoring them. The aim is not tolerance but full integration and acceptance.
- Use family stories and intergenerational narratives to inspire pride in their own culture and heritage.
- Talk about privilege and how that affects how people are treated in society.
- Teach children not to dismiss other people's experiences of racism, but be respectful of their feelings.
- Help children understand that racism is much more than just someone being mean or rude.
- Empower them with role play, tools and strategies to counter any racism they encounter.
- Maintain open-ended conversations and discussions to help you understand how children see themselves and others.
- Ask questions such as 'What makes you different? What makes you special?' that can help children explore self-identity.

Section V

Seven to Nine Years

In 1968, the day after the assassination of Martin Luther King, Jane Elliott, an educator and anti-racist activist, decided to address the problems of racial prejudice by dividing her third-grade class into groups on the basis of eye colour. All her students were white, and none of them could relate to the feeling of being a black person in America, so she wanted them to understand what discrimination feels like. As seen in the PBS Frontline documentary *A Class Divided*, Elliott showed how easy it was to turn her seven-year-old pupils into hatemongers by making the blue-eyed children the targets of discrimination by the 'better' brown-eyed children. After dividing the children, she told them that people with brown eyes were smarter, faster and better than those with blue eyes. She also gave the brown-eyed children other privileges. Soon the brown-eyed children became condescending towards their classmates, calling them 'stupid' and shunning them in the playground. The blue-eyed children became meek and withdrawn. Her blue eyes/brown eyes exercise, although also controversial, is considered a landmark in showing how environmental cues can shape our children's biases and reinforce our in-group memberships.

It confirmed that prejudice against members of the out-group is learned in children. However, if it is not addressed and unlearned, they can carry these biases throughout their lives.

By the age of seven, children have almost grown out of the egocentrism stage of development and can see different points of view. Children can now also understand that states are not fixed. So it is easier to discuss with them how identities can be fluid and transform rather than stay in a stationary state. According to Jean Piaget, this is the *concrete operational* stage of development that lasts until around 11 or 12 years of age, when children start forming more logical and rational thinking, even though they might still find it tricky to grasp some abstract concepts. There is some debate as to whether children have a clear understanding of categorisation and how different objects (or people) in the same category can also differ from each other and form subcategories. So they might still find it confusing how two brown people can be a Hispanic and an Indian, or how two black people might have different skin colours.

This is the age where children start forming a deeper sense of injustice in their own lives and so it is a good opportunity to start drawing parallels to the wider world. When children watch or see something about racial violence, it is important to speak with them in an honest manner, sensitive to their age, rather than trying to dismiss any such questions. Such conversations should be normalised. At this age, children should know and understand when racism is taking place, and how to counter and challenge it. It is important children understand that racism is not just explicit hate crimes but also works in implicit, insidious ways such as making fun of someone due to their skin colour or accent, or the way their hair looks, calling them names or excluding them because of their differences. Some examples of racism in the classroom and playground can include:

- Telling jokes directed against people from certain groups.
- Making fun of people's accents or names.
- Making fun of food, clothes or appearance of people.
- Stereotyping people from different cultural groups.
- Refusing to sit with or be in the same team as someone from a different group because of their skin colour, hair, religion or language.
- Making graffiti or signs that are offensive to people from certain cultural and ethnic groups.

Role play and group activities that help children take a scenario that they consider unfair and figure out how they could turn that into something fair can empower them, and remind them that they have the power to make change. But as parents, you can also discuss occasions where you did not handle a racial insult perfectly. These inadequacies in ourselves, talking about our fears and concerns, can help children understand that they do not have to be embarrassed when they suffer racism, that they can come and talk about it honestly, and in this way they learn to externalise rather than internalise any racism that comes their way.

This is also the age when children start forging a stronger sense of identity, with peer pressure becoming even more important. Some children might start rejecting their own culture and language that their parents speak at home in favour of what they see and hear at school, and what is in the majority. It is a really tricky and complex thing for immigrant parents of colour, in particular, to handle. Children can start internalising racism and oppression if we are not careful.

Children, much like adults, also learn to code-switch between home and school, speaking a different language inside and outside their homes, where they adopt different identities to fit in. Code-switching is the process of shifting from one language to another, or from one form of a language to another, in one conversation, or in different contexts. Many of us living and moving across borders and cultures are doing so: when I move seamlessly between English and Hindi in the same sentence, my English has an RP accent in the UK but slips back into the Indian nuances, drawl and twang when in India or when speaking to my parents. Mostly this happens unknowingly, but people can also sometimes deliberately adopt different personas to try and fit in with different social groups. This can create conflict and confusion, resulting in stress and anxiety from maintaining multiple identities. But there can be more serious implications if it involves switching between mannerisms and trying to conform to the beliefs and views children experience outside that may be contrary to those they follow at home. This might mean that they actively take on a new identity that is more in favour and makes them feel safer amongst their peers. Doing so can make them feel isolated within their own families. This is something that you, as a parent, have to actively watch out for through these years if you notice your child distancing themselves from the speech, dress and behaviours of their own family and community. A discussion about how it is OK to explore different aspects of ourselves, and to navigate racial, cultural, gender and other societal expectations around these different identities, can reassure the child that it is not always a choice of one or the other.

If you are a parent of colour, you should most certainly discuss the different forms of oppression that different people face based on their racial identities. For instance, brown people have faced racism in society too, much like black people, and continue to do so. But the racism that one group faces is not the same as another, nor is there a competition in who is more oppressed or who faces more racism. At this age, children can understand more about the colourism and anti-blackness that permeates some communities of colour. In these societies, due to centuries of colonialism, and internalised racism, people can believe that fair-skinned is superior, and in this way they can enable and support racism, especially against black people.

'Mixedness' becomes a more complex thing for families and for children to tackle at this age. It is coming to terms with how, on one hand, a child's position in society is secured by their proximity to whiteness (because of white parentage and lighter 'white-passing' skin colour), while also navigating the racism they might encounter in spaces where they still stand out as 'other'. This sense of divided identity starts becoming more crucial for children to understand around this age. Sometimes children might face racism even from within their own extended families, especially if whiteness is very deeply embedded in their own lives. This can include ignoring racism that affects the child, but also others around them. Denial is never good for healthy development. Our society is so fixated on clear boundaries and boxes that anyone who does not cleanly and clearly fit into their notion of 'black' or 'white', and is not one or the other but many, is perceived to be challenging. Here, talk to your child about multiple sides of their identity, and how it is OK to be all and not choose one or the other.

Children can move back and forth between different identities depending on which culture is more dominant in their family, which parent has more influence. If supported through this process, they will slowly get to the fluid stage where they can choose different forms of their identity. Rather than believing that they have to conform to certain stereotypes or internalise any racism that one part of their identity suffers, children can actively start naming themselves as part of the community that they feel most association and affiliation with rather than one they may be associated with because of their skin colour. Children have to understand that their identity and worth is not attached to one particular characteristic such as skin colour. And this can only happen if they also understand that no one should be defined by a caricature or stereotype they might have encountered in media or books, and so they cannot judge others either.

This is a critical age. By the age of nine, researchers say that 'when faced with counter-stereotypic information, children that showed highly stereotyped attitudes tended to forget that information, or, even more disturbingly, to distort it in memory to make their ideas consistent with their stereotyped beliefs'.[22] Frances Aboud in her book *Children and Prejudice*, published in 1988,[23] says that after the age of nine 'racial attitudes tend to stay constant unless the child experiences a life-changing event'.

Seven- to nine-year-olds are really moving into 'object permanence' where they start getting a sense that many things are going to stay the same. They will start understanding that their skin colour and their racial identity, as well as those of others, will stay the same. They are also looking for role models, for affinity groups where they can see more of themselves in positive ways, so that they can build pride in their own identity, but continue to experience diverse cultural experiences. This can be done through trips to museums, galleries, through books and movies, through speakers talking about different cultural experiences, through their curriculum, and through interaction with children and adults of different backgrounds. In doing so, they start developing affinities with other children outside their own racial and cultural identities, and making connections beyond the common race or ethnic background.

Once again, exploring their own skin, hair and eye colour, and talking about themselves and others, through words and images, will help children understand sameness and difference. This is the age when I started doing longer projects with P, in which she researched different topics related to history and identity. This helped her critical thinking, literacy and research skills while also encouraging her to foster empathy for people across different cultures. We visited the International Slavery Museum in Liverpool (they also have an excellent digital resource) and did a big project on slavery over the summer, collecting images and interviews with people, as well as using secondary resources. We also looked at art and artists from different eras to see how representation is based on societal norms and how stereotypes can be reinforced through images. This is a good exercise as children have to navigate visual imagery all around them, which often perpetuates harmful stereotypes.

Q 8: Why can't I use the n-word?

Some of the parents I have worked with have talked with me about the use of the 'n-word' and how they have found it difficult to explain to their young children why they should not be using it, while it is being used in songs and popular culture by both black and white artists. The conversation around any of these words has to be more about 'let's talk about what is inappropriate about this word', 'here is what is problematic', rather than an outright 'just do not use that word'. When we give an outright ultimatum the child is more likely to rebel because they think of the word as forbidden and edgy. Believe me. I know from experience! When P was young, and I was a single parent working full-time in a very demanding academic position, and generally just juggling millions of things, there were times when the easiest fallback position was to say 'Just don't use that word because I said so.' It did not work. And in all honesty, I didn't expect it to. If you have already been having conversations around race with your child from a young age, and talked to them about civil rights and slavery, then it will be an easier conversation to have to explain to them that the n-word is a racial label that was commonly used by white people to describe black people during slavery and segregation. Even today, when it is sometimes used with a slightly modified spelling (such as 'nigga') as a term of endearment, especially when black people are referring to other black people, it is impossible to separate it from its historical context tangled up in violence and intimidation. No matter if the child is white or black, the use of certain words carries a lot of historical baggage. Using it now, even with a different spelling, dismisses these past experiences of black people and the oppression they faced, and it makes it seem that racism is a thing of the past. It is not.

You can find children's books and other material that show how this word is problematic and was used in a derogatory manner. The children's book *Can I Touch Your Hair?: Poems of Race, Mistakes, and Friendship* includes a poem called 'The N-Bomb' that says that no matter how the word is spelled, it is still 'a spit in the face' of the ancestors who fought against oppression for so long.

Giving concrete historical examples of how the word was used by people who committed violent crimes and were motivated by hatred of black people can make it much clearer to children. The word was used in minstrel songs (some of which are still sung today with some of these verses removed) by white people to mock black people. It is also connected with the lynchings, the Jim Crow segregation and the Ku Klux Klan. Professor Neal A. Lester from Arizona State University says that 'No degree of appropriating can rid it of that bloodsoaked history.'[24] He also believes that there is a double standard around the word because it is allowed for some to use but not for others. This causes a lot of problems because of a heightened racially charged emotional response.

While you are having these conversations with your children, you still have to remember that they are children. Sometimes it is not possible to have a lengthy debate about the cultural and social context around certain words and terms, and how and where they should be used. Sometimes you might not know the context yourself. But this can be an opportunity to learn together. It is okay to say: 'Actually I don't know all this myself but let us look up some resources and we can find out together.'

You can start talking more with your children about words and language that really matter as their vocabulary becomes more sophisticated. The meanings of words are shaped by context. And all words are shaped by their historical significance, and the right way to use them should also be determined by the context in which they are being used. Taking hip-hop as an example, or *Huckleberry Finn*, and discussing with the child whether the use of this word is appropriate in these cases opens up a critical discussion around language and racism, and it creates a platform for self-reflection and thoughtful action.

Enobong Essien writing on Book Riot in January 2020[25] talks about her sister, a black teacher in a predominantly white school with only two black children in her class of 30:

> The class are studying the John Steinbeck classic *Of Mice and Men*. Like many great American classics, the Black characters in this book are often referred to as the n-word and other offensive names. If anyone is caught using the word in the school my sister works at, they risk expulsion. My sister didn't relax those rules for her classroom.
>
> At the beginning of her lesson, she handed each student in her class a sticker to place in the front of their book. This note is a reminder to every student that the use of the n-word and other such words is a hate crime and will result in expulsion if the word is used in her classroom. Even when they are reading the book out loud as a class, she is the only person

allowed to use the word. Everyone else must say 'the n-word'. They can say the word in their heads, but they are not to use it out loud. All racial slurs continue to be banned in her literature class, regardless of whether they're in a book or not.

This might seem like a drastic step to some. For me, this seems like a great opportunity for children to recognise that literature and language evolve and there are some words that have racist associations and are not appropriate for us to use any more. I also personally believe that a conversation around why this word is problematic has to go side by side with this approach.

If you are a parent of a younger child and find any such words while reading a book, you can just verbally edit out the text at that stage. There has been much debate about whether children's texts should be edited or censored but we have to remember that children's books have been written by adults, and they bring their own biased views and stereotypes to them. Many of the books that we consider classics now depict black and brown people in a very racist and stereotypical way.

It is your responsibility to discuss any racially charged words with your children because language shapes stereotypes and bias. It is your responsibility to curate your child's view of reality, and their understanding of what their world should look like. Words have the power to hurt and so children also have the power to not use these words any more.

Q 9: Why are people still racist?

As you are doing this work with your children, they will get the message that racism is bad, and everyone should be treated equally. Why then are adults still racist? Why does racism still persist? It is a million-dollar question. It still persists because some people are not ready to give up their position of privilege, even when they hold it unknowingly. People are afraid of losing their own place in society.

It is important to introduce the idea of historical oppression as a combination of prejudice and institutional power that creates a system that regularly and severely discriminates against some groups and benefits other groups. And it is important to discuss the idea of power and privilege with children so that they understand how small acts, such as jokes about someone's looks or accent based on racial distinction, can also lead to bigger systemic problems. These systemic ideologies persist, and inform people's stereotypes and biases.

Many people grow up with the idea of whiteness being the norm and without much direct contact with people of colour. Since much of their information is coming from secondary sources, from books or television or movies, they see casual jokes and remarks made about people from minority ethnic communities and they start believing that in some way they are not as good, they are not as clever, they are worth less. They will package all this information up subconsciously as stereotypes. This then affects how they treat these people who they consider to be different from them, and less deserving of the same opportunities that they themselves have.

When we start talking about equality in society, some white people might feel like opportunities are being taken away from them and given to others. Some people might not understand that this is making a better society for everyone and as a result they might become more prejudiced against those who they are now having to share their resources with. Talking about racism, and reducing discrimination is not an anti-white bias but some people might think that it is reducing their opportunities.

For example, six chocolates are divided, and one child takes five chocolates and another child is only left with one. This isn't equality. Or fairness. So all the chocolates are collected together and divided equally, so that both children now have three. The child who previously had five chocolates now feels that they have lost, and the other child has gained. But what has happened is that now both children have an equal number of chocolates, as should have been the case to start off with. The child who had five has not lost out and the other has not gained in the real sense, because it is unfair for the two children to have an unequal number of chocolates in the first place.

Some people might contribute to racist beliefs and systems but not consider themselves at all racist. Racism is not just name-calling or acts of racial violence. Racism also comes from simple acts such as only buying and reading books by white authors. These are often unintentional acts stemming from unconscious biases that only white writers make significant cultural contributions, that they do better work. This still creates a system of advantage for white people, and dismisses the contribution made by writers of colour.

Not speaking up when you see any acts of racial exclusion or staying silent when you hear a racist joke is also a form of racism, and facilitates the persistence of racism in our society. Thinking that white people are the norm, that you do not carry any privileges as a white person, believing that skin colour does not matter – all these also contribute to racism in society.

To stop people being racist, and to interrupt racism, we all have to be very intentional about it. We have to work hard to break out of stereotypes and we have to be mindful of our words and language. This takes time, effort and energy and some people are not prepared to put in the work.

Q 10: A black child at school called me rude names. Are they being racist towards me?

Are only white people racist?

Everyone can be prejudiced. Not just white people.

But racism is much more than this.

Racism cannot be understood without the context of history. The idea of racial hierarchies was invented and propagated by white Europeans as they started sailing to distant lands around the 1400s, interacting with indigenous populations on a large scale. They created the idea of racial hierarchies where white was superior and black people were at the bottom. These ideas and stereotypes of indigenous populations were justified through the belief that they were biologically inferior to white Europeans. As Europeans began to conquer, enslave and otherwise dominate or exploit different populations around the world, they also started to write about their experiences. Art that was created around this time and that we see in museums around us is also based on their views and perceptions of non-Europeans. For example, we see many paintings of white men with black people as servants, or images where a white man is seen as a saviour. As print media started becoming widespread, these stereotypes became more widely known and part of popular culture. By the end of the nineteenth century, Europeans dominated the world financially and politically, and the European populace generally believed that their rule over people from far-off lands was justified because they were inherently superior.

This means that racism still exists as a system of disadvantage for those groups of people who were considered inferior and never had the same opportunities. So racism is rooted in this belief that one race (or skin colour) is superior to another, even as race is a social construct. Therefore, while black people can be prejudiced against white people, especially in places where they are in the majority, this cannot be termed racism.

We have also seen prejudices against large groups of people because of their ethnic backgrounds that result in ethnic cleansing, where a certain subgroup is systematically forced out of a certain area based on their culture or religion. Once again, there is an underlying belief that this group is inferior to another. This happened with Jews in Nazi Germany, and this is happening with Uyghur Muslims in China. The aim is to create ethnically homogeneous areas or states. Usually this is targeted at the minority ethnic communities and the indigenous populations and based on power imbalance and oppression. There is academic debate over whether this is also a form of racism or not, and it remains a nuanced discussion.

Explain to your child that when a black child is mean or rude, that does not mean that they are exhibiting racism. Yes, bullying of any form should not be ignored, and it should definitely be addressed, but calling this racism dismisses the legacy and history of oppression and ignores the systemic and institutional racism that people of colour experience.

Q 11: Are white people really bad? Are we bad people?

No. Racism was not your idea. You do not have to defend it. You do not have to feel guilty about it. Because that will not solve racism. But racism exists. White privilege exists. Some white people do abuse this power.

You have the power to learn about it, acknowledge it, and do something about it. Staying silent is not the solution. Not talking about racism is not the answer.

There are good people and there are bad people, of all skin colours. But skin colour makes a difference in how people see you, and how you see the world. As a white person, you are safer, and the societally accepted norm, unlike many black or brown children. You are part of the majority. And that gives you the power to change things.

CHECKLIST

◆ Keep diversifying children's reading lists, bringing in more challenging texts translated from other languages that are less likely to have cultural stereotypes.

◆ Continue to support their curiosity about their own identities and those of others through active engagement and questions.

◆ Allow them to explore different identities until they become comfortable with multiple notions of identity and do not feel the need to switch between different identities at home and amongst friends.

◆ Help your child to understand the difference between respectful and abusive behaviour.

◆ Talk to your child about the ways that racism can manifest in the classroom and the playground, through jokes and name-calling.

◆ Help your children understand that while any form of bullying is bad and should be addressed, not all forms of bullying are racism.

◆ Ask open-ended questions such as 'What would you do if someone was being racist on your bus?' and talk through appropriate responses and actions.

- Encourage them to share their feelings about race and racism without feeling embarrassed or ashamed of not knowing something or thinking a certain way.
- If your child is hurt by racist behaviour, do not try to deny, explain away or make excuses for their experience.
- If your child exhibits racist behaviour, don't panic. Instead sit down with them and have a calm conversation about why it is not acceptable and what its implications are.
- Support and empower your child in externalising rather than internalising any racial remarks they hear.
- Explain to them that words and language have power, and we have the power to not use words that are offensive and can hurt people belonging to different cultural and ethnic groups.
- Discuss equality and fairness, and that equality is when everyone is treated fairly, not necessarily the same.
- Ask questions such as: 'How did you feel about what you saw on the news? What did you think about it?'
- Through scenarios and role play help them in

understanding what is fair and what is unfair, and empower them in knowing how they can change things.

◆ Ask them questions such as 'What would equality look like to you in your school and at home?' and 'Have you noticed if everyone is treated equally in your classroom?' and then discuss any racial stereotyping and differences that come up in their responses.

Ten to Twelve Years

This is the age when strong emotions surface and children can get very angry about any injustice they see around them. This is also when they start forging new friendships, facing more outside influences, start separating themselves from you, and start having very strong opinions about everything. This is when lines of communication have to stay open.

The work continues.

Children start forming a deeper sense of morality and social justice, especially if you have engaged them in such conversations from a young age. Around the age of nine or ten, children form a sense of *autonomous morality* or *moral relativism*, which means that they can see morality from other people's point of view too, and that people may differ in how they understand and approach the same moral situation or problem. So it becomes easier for them to learn how to externalise any racism directed towards them rather than internalising it because they understand that how they feel about themselves does not have to be governed by what others think of them. They can separate people's views of them from how they see their own identity ('*They think of me like this, but I think of myself in a different way*'). Children will continue to show the impact of any learned stereotyping and dislike of other racial and cultural groups, but they also become more capable of evaluating information more critically, and able to understand how differences in perspectives shape people's identities.

Their idea of what is fair and unfair is expanding as they move out of the egocentrism phase of development. Children also reach a stage of 'reciprocity', according to Piaget, where they understand that we are all human, but also members of many different subgroups according to race, language, religion, gender, etc. and so we have same but also different needs. This can help children to understand the different forms of oppression that different subgroups face, and how our belonging to different groups shapes our privileges.

Children reach these different phases of moral development at different rates. According to Lawrence Kohlberg,[26] a developmental theorist, children at this stage are progressing through a conventional level of morality. In the first stage of this developmental phase, children start grasping that their moral decisions will be judged by other influential group members. Because they want to be considered a good person and be in favour in their peer group, or with those who are influential in their lives such as teachers or parents, their decisions will be based on whether their actions will be approved by these people. So their peer groups, and what they see and hear from you and their teachers, matter a lot. Their moral framework is being determined by what you, their peer group and their teachers consider acceptable. And so their framework of racial justice is still shaped by their reference groups, which remain very important.

As they move through this developmental phase into teenage years, children can start understanding a notion of morality which is good for the majority of people and society in general. This is called *social-order-maintaining orientation* as per Kohlberg's framework, where children can understand that acting in a certain way is not beneficial to the society while also breaking the law. Children of this age start forming the notion of *morality of cooperation* where they realise that people have to work together to create a harmonious society towards a common good. And they can understand that the morality of a situation also depends on the intentionality and not just the outcome, so when children say that they did not mean to be racist or hurt someone, you can talk to them about why their intent and their action is as important as the outcome.

If children have had a rigorous racial education from a young age, they may already be moving into a stage of moral development where they understand what their most important beliefs and values are, and that it is important to act in accordance with these ideological beliefs. They can see that laws and rules, while important, are shaped by context and majority, that they cannot be followed rigidly, and that they need to be reinterpreted at certain times to make sure that they are achieving social justice. And this is why we see our pre-teenagers and teenagers rebelling and breaking the law, as they test which laws are flexible and weigh up their own ideological beliefs against pre-determined rules.

Children need more opportunities for critical thinking. Asking them questions such as 'What do you think about this issue?', 'Why do you think this person behaved in this way?', 'What would you have done in this situation?', 'Why do you think this is not fair?' and 'What more can we do to make this better?' will open up a space for non-judgemental and honest conversations and learning. Do your best to meet each child where they are, developmentally and emotion-ally, because every child is different. It is important to hear and validate their questions, fears and emotions, and not dismiss their views, thoughts and experiences. Once again, no one has all the answers, but at this age children will be taking more of a lead, doing research, finding out information. Use this as a learning experi-ence for yourself and for them, something you can work towards together.

Eminé Rushton, editor at *Oh* magazine, shared with me:

'We have always questioned as a family why there are no characters from different ethnicities in shows the children may watch or black characters in the recommended reading from school. We talk about black stereotypes and whether the black kids talk or act or dress like the white kids, and if so, why, and if not, why not, or why the black kid in the show always seems to be a certain "type" of character (often precocious, cheeky, funny). Who created and wrote these shows? What impact might that have?'

This sounds like a great approach to working together with children in unravelling how systemic racism can affect what they watch and read, which people have opportunities and how people are represented, which stories are written and heard.

This is also the time when your own values and beliefs will get challenged a lot, and so it might be important for you to go back to reflecting on your own biases. As children start questioning authority, they will quickly point out and notice if you are not 'walking the talk'. It is important to show that you are not adopting race education merely for self-gratification and performativity. Children will pick up on cues.

- Are you engaged in your community?
- Are you drawing knowledge from your own community?

- Are you demonstrating that you are also reading diverse literature that pushes back against colonialism and oppression?
- Are you taking part in protests and actively being anti-racist yourself?
- Are you taking every opportunity to challenge racist behaviours, practices and policies, demonstrate kindness, and stand up for every person's right to be treated with dignity and respect?

Around this age, children can start having a deeper understanding of racism in all forms. They can differentiate racism from other forms of unfair treatment. They can also understand the difference between interpersonal and institutional and social racism. This distinction is important for them in order to develop appropriate tools for building more resilient anti-racist thinking and behaviour. When young people start to understand fully how cultural and institutional racism works, they can also understand how superiority and privilege can be internalised and normalised. And they can start rejecting any internalised white racism and develop a stronger anti-racist ideology. Children of colour can also understand how internalised oppression works as they become more interested in their own history and identity. This can aid them in de-internalising any racism they face and countering it with positive messages.

Sometimes, as children carve out their identities

and ideologies, and move through this phase where the opinions of reference groups outside their homes are growing in importance, they can sometimes fall back into stereotypes and biases that you have challenged from a young age. They might exhibit behaviour that is a manifestation of their internalised privilege or oppression in the form of anger and bullying towards others who are weaker than them. It is hard but do not despair. Sometimes all it takes is to sit down with them and have an empathetic conversation. Psychologist Beverly Daniel Tatum talks about a 'spiral staircase' where as children move through the phases of development and identity formation, they can sometimes get bumped back down because race and racism is always present in society.[27] But even when this happens, children have a more empowered sense of what they could be, what is possible, and they have more perspective on the situation than if they hadn't even started climbing this staircase in the first place. Once they have started this journey, it is easier for children to see that there is a better way to be, and that they can be an ally even if it's challenging.

Children are looking for connections, for the groups that can affirm their identities. For minority ethnicity children it can be very empowering to find other children who share similar experiences and to have these affinity groups where they feel a true sense of belonging. For white children, if they are in the majority, they have to be mindful of such silos, where they do not experience any cultural diversity. Talk to them again about power and privilege. And about when is it their responsibility to stand up, and call out racism they see in their communities, classrooms and playgrounds. What kind of words can they use to challenge such behaviours? What might such situations look like? When is it OK to intervene? It is important we teach them the right vocabulary and terminology. And also when they might need to call someone else in power if they are not equipped to deal with a situation.

Some parents have expressed concern that talking about race and racial injustice can make our children more fearful and aware of their differences. But we can do this in a very positive way. We can use it to empower children rather than making them fearful of their place in the world. So rather than them feeling anxious about being stereotyped, we can help them feel confident in their own identity, and that they belong completely, and that they can stand up to any unfairness.

Finally, encourage them into action. Young people have a great capacity to commit to and help organise creative anti-racism and social justice action in their community. Are there biased textbooks in their school? Are there racist programmes on the local radio station? Does the local library not have enough diverse books for all age groups? It was adolescents and young adults who were the heart of the great civil rights movement of the sixties. Knowing about positive role models and organisations who are working for change will make children confident that they can change things too if they want to. Work with them to write letters to the local council or to their school raising any racial inequality they have noticed. When young people know they have a voice in their community, they are empowered to help resolve issues of injustice. Rather than being part of the problem, they can be part of a solution. Encourage them to volunteer where they have to face their own privileges. Take part in protests and anti-racism marches with them where they can design posters.

Parents can model behaviours that we want to encourage in our children, such as fairness and social justice. We feel more comfortable pointing out sexist behaviour and gender biases, but we often choose to ignore those linked to race and colour. By highlighting strong role models from different racial and ethnic origins, we can empower our children. When they feel empowered, they feel more confident about their own race and their identity.

EXERCISE

Have a deeper discussion about the different forms of racism with your children: interpersonal, institutional and structural racism.

Interpersonal Racism: When a white person uses misinformation and stereotypes about another group to carry out harassment, exclusion, discrimination, hate or violence, they are committing an act of interpersonal racism.

Questions to discuss:

- Have you heard about or seen any acts of interpersonal racism recently?
- What does interpersonal racism do?[28]
- Why does it happen?

Institutional Racism: Things such as segregation, bias and discrimination in the housing market, in education and employment are racism at an institutional level that affects opportunities and the progress of people of colour. If a teacher does not give due weight and consideration to the views of students of colour in the classroom, if most or all teachers in a school are white, and if children of colour are disciplined more harshly, which affects their work performance and exam results, then this is a form of institutional racism.

Questions to discuss:

- How can institutional racism happen in your school?
- Can you think of any other examples of institutional racism?
- How does it benefit white people?
- How does it harm people of colour?

Structural Racism: This is the intersection of inter-personal and institutional racism that limits life choices and opportunities for people of colour. It is also reinforced by pervasive stereotypes and negative representations of people of colour and immigrants.

Questions to discuss:

- How does cultural appropriation[29] link to structural racism?
- Have you seen any examples of structural racism recently?
- What do you think we need to do to make sure that we are not contributing to structural racism?

Q 12: How can I be a good ally?

Sometimes merely showing support can be enough. For instance, if a child is sitting alone on a bench in the playground because they are being excluded or called names because of their skin colour, sometimes allyship can be just going and sitting with them when no one else does. Being an ally is so much about kindness and compassion for others, despite our differences. But in doing anti-racism work, caring is not enough. We have to also actively challenge and counter racist views.

This is the age when children should be moving from awareness to action.

Develop a range of different scenarios and discuss with your child what action they would take in each scenario and why.

Examples:

1. A friend makes fun of another student because of their skin colour.
2. Another student who you don't know makes fun of a student because of their skin colour, calling them names or writing insulting messages about them.
3. Two students make fun of another student's accent or their food, or their traditional clothing.

Sample scenario:

Emma and Tracey sit next to each other in class. Emma thinks that all black people are stupid. She tells Tracey this and refuses to sit with her in the next lesson.

Emma is white. Tracey is black.

1. How would you feel if you were Tracey?
2. What do you think of Emma's behaviour?
3. Why do you think Emma behaved in this way?
4. What could Tracey do in this situation?
5. What would you do in this situation?

Possible actions can include:

- Intervene directly
- Walk away
- Ask an adult or teacher for help
- Talk to the person in private

Discuss with your child what they would choose to do, and how, and more importantly why. Think about the outcome in each scenario.

Being an anti-racist and an ally involves clarifying your own motivation. Ask your child:

'Why do you want to do this?'

'What would be the ideal outcome?'
'What is your goal?'

And then understand the level of commitment they have. Does it only extend to friends and close family? Or are they conscious that being an anti-racist and an ally means supporting anyone who is oppressed and marginalised?

Discuss these points with your child:

1. Being an ally is an action. You cannot define and label yourself an ally. It is up to the people of colour to consider and designate you an ally. However, you can demonstrate through action and words that you are committed to being one.

2. Being an ally is not for performativity or for fame. It is to decentre yourself and shine the light on those who are less privileged than you. Remember an ally is not the hero but the sidekick.

3. As an ally you will make some mistakes. It is no reason to get embarrassed or give up. This is a commitment that you make. And you are accountable.

4. Allies keep learning and educating themselves.

Things young (white) people can do to be a good ally:

1. Acknowledge white privilege. Not acknowledging white privilege is really the first sign of white privilege. Accept that it gives you some opportunities that others may not have. Think about how you can leverage this privilege to give a nudge to those who are carrying the burden of racism.

2. Support those who are being targeted whether you know them or not. Ask them if they are OK. Ask them if they need any help. Do not question their experience, or tell them that 'It was probably nothing', or 'Are you sure?' or even 'I am sure they didn't mean anything.' Make sure they know they are not alone.

3. Do not take part in any activities such as jokes, bullying or name-calling that target others because of their differences.

4. Stand up and let the aggressors know that it is not OK to behave in this manner. Tell them what the outcome of their actions is, and how it is hurtful.

5. Getting help about an issue of racism is never 'snitching', so do inform a trusted adult, whether a teacher or parent or another carer.

6. Learn to take the time to get to know people before making assumptions and judgements about them or assigning stereotypes. Try and engage with diverse groups of children in your class, especially those who are in the minority.

7. Do not share widely other people's stories of racism without seeking their permission. It is not your story to tell.

8. Name the racism. If you see or hear something racist, call it out.

CHECKLIST

- Create more opportunities for critical thinking and discussions.
- Continue to diversify children's education at home, critically discussing maps, literature and history, their context and their authorship.
- Continue introducing children to family stories and personal histories to inspire a sense of pride in their own culture and community.
- Discuss the different forms of racism, and help children in recognising these around them in books, media, the playground and the classroom.
- Discuss with your children what being a good ally really means.
- Empower children with strategies on how

they can stand up against any racism that they see and hear.

♦ Create more opportunities for them to engage in activities that support them in recognising and acknowledging their own privileges.

♦ Make sure that you model the behaviours that you expect from them: volunteer, engage with a diverse community, and move past tokenistic allyship.

Epilogue

This hasn't been an easy book to write. This is not easy work. It has forced me to relive some of my own traumas and experiences, through writing about them but also while talking to other parents of colour. Parenting is not an easy thing to do anyway. I have raised a grown-up daughter and in doing so I have realised that I have made many mistakes. I am not a parenting expert. In fact, I find the whole idea of a parenting expert quite bizarre. But my personal position and lived experience, and my academic research, have given me the conviction to write about this subject. I write this book in the spirit of community and collaboration, learning and growing together.

I have faced racial abuse on social media for writing and talking about this subject. I have been told that 'you are starting a cult', 'you are indoctrinating our children', 'you are moaning about race again', or even that I should go back home where I come from, with abusive words for my children, and how they will suffer for my misdemeanours, and much, much worse. I often sat in front of the computer reading these messages, thinking of how important and crucial it is that we talk honestly and openly about race and racism, and how difficult it is to do so. I have never felt more vulnerable than when writing this book. But also never more driven by how urgent this is.

Some final thoughts in our crusade to raise anti-racist children:

1. Use explicit proactive language, giving very clear cues to children about skin colour and why some words and actions are racist. For example:

   'I don't like this video that you are watching. It is racist towards Indian people.'

   'Here in this newspaper, this black man has been shown as being bad and the journalist has made a guess that he is looting. But the journalist does not know this. Black people can both be good and bad. White people can be both good and bad too. Being good or bad does not depend on someone's skin colour.'

   'Parents and children make a family but their skin colours don't have to match to make a family.

Sometimes children can be in-between. It is not skin colour but love that makes a family.'

'There are more black people in this neighbour-hood than in ours because in the past some white people did not want black people to be living near them. This meant that black people did not feel safe living in some neighbourhoods and they decided to move into places where they felt safe together as a community. Sometimes this is how racism works too because it creates separate spaces for black and white people.'

2. Explicitly name race when reading books with your toddler and pre-schooler. This might seem very forced but it helps you move away from a colour-blind approach, and it becomes natural slowly. There are some good books that I have added in the resources section that do this very well.

'Look, this baby has brown skin like yours and lovely brown hair like Mummy. She could be black or Indian or Hispanic. And look, this one has more pinkish skin that is called white with green eyes. Did you notice that we all have differ-ent skin, hair and eye colours?'

You don't have to do it every time. Also you don't have to do it when you are meeting friends and strangers. But normalising conversations around race and difference in skin colour is very important from a young age.

3. Remember, if we don't say something, kids will fill in the gaps with their own interpretations. So while reading, it is always worth pointing out to them that even if in the image there are only white people in the café or shop, this is not always the case in real life. There would be people of all skin colours, and black people also go to cafés and the theatre. Or children might assume that it is only people who live in India who wear a sari, for instance, and it is important to remind them that they could be living anywhere and wearing a sari. That is linked to a person's cultural background and people of all cultures live in Britain or America. Also, not all Indian women wear a sari. Or go to a temple. Not all Muslim women wear a niqab. We must actively help our children address and move away from stereotypes.

4. As parents, we have to learn and unlearn every day. Keep working on your implicit biases, your words, your actions. It takes a lot of

courage and self-reflection to acknowledge our ingrained cultural conditioning and disrupt the prejudices we have learned and absorbed through our lives. Sit with the discomfort.

As parents, we often do not want to expose our children to uncomfortable and inconvenient truths. This might be motivated by preserving their innocence and saving them from any anguish. But if you do not educate them about racism, and do not talk explicitly about its impact, they will never be immune from the internalisation of white privilege and superiority. So even though this might be uncomfortable, we have to teach our children that they cannot accept injustice, that they have the power to change things, that they can leverage and manipulate their white privilege to create a better and fairer society.

Recent research published in PsyArXiv conducted by psychologist Sylvia Perry and colleagues at Northwestern University[30] shows that even as most white parents feel discomfort while talking about race, children's (and parents') implicit racial attitudes significantly decreased from pre- to post-conversation. This means that any conversation helps us, as parents, to reflect on our own unconscious biases and attitudes even as we support our children in becoming anti-racist. The findings suggest that the discomfort that white adults often experience when openly discussing racial issues need not be a barrier to progress. The researchers show that it could even be helpful for white children to see their parents model discomfort with racist acts, and to hear their own experiences.

All parents have to do this work, in different ways, to prevent internalised racialisation or oppression, and to make sure our children grow up confident of their identities and place in the world.

Talking about racism is creating happier, healthier and more hopeful children. And any discomfort has to be worth it.

Notes

1   BAME stands for 'black, Asian and minority ethnic', and is
    widely used in the UK along with BME ('black and minority
    ethnic'). In the US, mostly 'people of colour' or PoC is used,
    a term first cited in the Oxford English Dictionary in 1796.
    Today, BIPOC is becoming more common, which stands for
    'black, indigenous and people of colour', expanded to include
    voices that were not normally being heard. All these terms are
    problematic, in my view, as they homogenise disparate groups
    of people. Fitting all of them into one acronym seems tone-
    deaf and not letting them take up space on their own. But this
    is how data is currently aggregated. In this book I have used
    'people of colour'.
2   Brigitte Vittrup, 'Color Blind or Color Conscious? White
    American Mothers' Approaches to Racial Socialization',
    Journal of Family Issues 39.3 (2018): 668–92.
3   Lucinda Platt, 'Ethnicity and Family: Relationships within
    and between Ethnic Groups' (Institute for Social &
    Economic Research, University of Essex, 2009), https://
    www.equalityhumanrights.com/sites/default/files/
    research-paper-ethnicity-and-family-relationships-within-and-
    between-ethnic-groups.pdf.
4   Devah Pager, Bruce Western and Bart Bonikowski,
    'Discrimination in a Low-Wage Labor Market: A
    Field Experiment', *American Sociological Review* 74.5
    (2009): 777–99.

5   Emil Jeyaratnam, 'Twelve Charts on Race and Racism in Australia', The Conversation, 27 November 2018, https://theconversation.com/twelve-charts-on-race-and-racism-in-australia-105961.

6   Research conducted by Kim Parker, Juliana Menasce Horowitz, Rich Morin and Mark Hugo Lopez for Pew Research Centre.

7   Dalton Conley quoted in 'Ask the Experts: What is the Difference Between Race and Ethnicity?', PBS website, www.pbs.org/race/000_About/002_04-experts-03-02.htm.

8   Bianca Gonzalez-Sobrino and Devon R. Goss, 'Exploring the Mechanisms of Racialization Beyond the Black–White Binary', Ethnic and Racial Studies 42.4 (2019): 505–10.

9   Harry Brod, 'Work Clothes and Leisure Suits: The Class Basis and Bias of the Men's Movement', in Men's Lives, ed. Michael S. Kimmel and Michael Messner (New York: Macmillan, 1989), p. 280.

10 Pragya Agarwal, Sway: Unravelling Unconscious Bias (London: Bloomsbury, 2020).

11 Halsey, Twitter post, 3 June 2020, https://twitter.com/halsey/status/1268048747738497024.

12 Colourism, a term coined by the activist Alice Walker in 1982, is the bias that 'white is beautiful', creating the aspiration for white skin.

13 Mathew Knowles was a visiting Professor here and discussed this study conducted by his students on SiriusXM Urban View with Clay Cane in June 2019.

14 One of the most famous cases of the twentieth century is the writer Anatole Broyard, who passed as white for decades to avoid facing discrimination from the white literary and publishing world. He hid his origins and identity even from his own children, who did not know the truth until Broyard's death in 1990.

15 Salman Akhtar, ed., The New Motherhoods: Patterns of Early Child Care in Contemporary Culture (Lanham, MA: Rowman & Littlefield Publishers, 2015).

16 Kinzler, K. D., and Spelke, E. S. (2011). 'Do infants show social preferences for people differing in race?', Cognition, 119 (1), 1–9.

17 Dr Beverly Daniel Tatum in her book *Why Are All the Black Kids Sitting Together in the Cafeteria?: And Other Conversations About Race* (New York: Basic Books, 2017), speaks of anti-blackness as a smog.

18 A tignon (pronounced 'teeyon') is a headdress.

19 Or any such role model. We had been reading *Frida Kahlo* from the *Little People, Big Dreams* series at home at the time.

20 Gregory S. Barsh, 'What controls variation in human skin color?', *PLoS Biology* 1.1 (2003): e27.

21 Credit for describing the relationship between latitude and skin colour in modern humans is usually ascribed to an Italian geographer, Renato Biasutti, whose widely reproduced 'skin colour maps' show the correlation of darker skin with equatorial proximity. More work has been done on this since. However, an important caveat is that we do not know how patterns of UV radiation have changed over time. Also, we do not know when skin colour is likely to have evolved, with multiple migrations out of Africa and extensive mingling of genes over the last 500,000 years: see Alan Templeton, 'Out of Africa again and again', *Nature* 416 (2002): 45–51.

22 Rebecca S. Bigler and Lynn S. Liben, 'A Cognitive-Developmental Approach to Racial Stereotyping and Reconstructive Memory in Euro-American Children', *Child Development* 64.5 (1993): 1507–18.

23 Frances Aboud, *Children and Prejudice* (Cambridge, MA: Basil Blackwell, 1988).

24 Neal A. Lester interviewed by Sean Price, 'Straight Talk About the N-Word', *Tolerance*, Issue 40, Fall 2011, www.tolerance. org/magazine/fall-2011/straight-talk-about-the-nword.

25 Enobong Essien, 'The N-Word: Confronting Racial Slurs in Literature', *Book Riot*, 27 January 2020, www.bookriot.com/ racial-slurs-in-literature.

26 Kohlberg, Lawrence (1981). *Essays on Moral Development, Vol. I: The Philosophy of Moral Development*. San Francisco, CA:

27 Tatum, B. D. (1992). 'Talking about race, learning about racism: The application of racial identity development theory in the classroom', *Harvard Educational Review*, 62(1), 1–24.

28 It affects the mental and physical well-being of those who

are targeted, with heightened stress and anxiety which over a period of time can lead to cardiovascular diseases. It reinforces institutional racism. It breaks down a harmonious multicultural society.

29   Cultural appropriation is when a white person takes an element from the culture of a minority group without a deep understanding of their culture, without any connection or permission, and specifically for monetary gain.

30   Perry, S., Skinner, A., Abaied, J. L., Osnaya, A. and Waters, S. (2020, May 18). 'Exploring how Parent-Child Conversations about Race influence Children's Implicit Biases', PsyArXiv doi:10.31234/osf.io/3xdg8.

Further Resources

Book Recommendations

Here the recommended reading age for younger children is around zero to seven years, and the next group is for eight years and over. But once again these are merely tentative guidelines, as children vary in their reading comprehension and maturity. I have tried to recommend books that bring diverse families and backgrounds from around the world into children's lives without conforming to archaic stereotypes. In fact, I have actively tried to recommend books that shatter these generalised assumptions about different cultures and ethnicities.

Books for young children
Two Eyes, a Nose and a Mouth by Roberta Grobel
    Intrater
I'm Your Peanut Butter Big Brother by Selina Alko

Black Girl Magic: A Poem by Mahogany L. Browne

Trailblazer: The Story of Ballerina Raven Wilkinson by Leda Schubert

Abuela's Special Letters (Sofia Martinez) by Jacqueline Jules and Kim Smith

Free as a Bird: The Story of Malala by Lina Maslo

Why Are They Kneeling? by Lauren J. Coleman

Thirteen Ways of Looking at a Black Boy by Tony Medina

Boonoonoonous Hair! by Olive Senior

On Our Street: Our First Talk About Poverty (The World Around Us) by Jillian Roberts and Jaime Casap

Lila and the Crow by Gabrielle Grimard

My Hair Is a Garden by Cozbi A. Cabrera

Tell Me Who You Are: Shaping Our Stories of Race, Culture, and Identity by Winona Guo and Priya Vulchi

31 Fantastic Adventures in Science: Women Scientists of India by Nandita Jayaraj and Aashima Friedog

The Mega Magic Hair Swap! by Rochelle Humes

The Proudest Blue by Ibtihaj Muhammad

My Hair by Hannah Lee

The Undefeated by Kwame Alexander

Little Leaders: Bold Women in Black History by Vashti Harrison

I Am Enough by Grace Byers

Sulwe by Lupita Nyong'o, illustrated by Vashti Harrison

A Is for Activist by Innosanto Nagara

Not My Idea: A Book about Whiteness by Anastasia Higginbotham

Something Else by Kathryn Cave and Chris Riddell

Colour of People by Maurício Negro

Mixed by Arree Chung

The Power Book: What Is it, Who Has It, and Why? by Claire Saunders, Hazel Songhurst, Georgia Amson-Bradshaw, Minna Salami and Mik Scarlet

Something Happened in Our Town: A Child's Story about Racial Injustice by Marianne Celano, Marietta Collins and Ann Hazzard

Layla's Head Scarf by Miriam Cohen

Ada Twist, Scientist by Andrea Beaty

Brown Girl Dreaming by Jacqueline Woodson

Grandpa, Is Everything Black Bad? by Sandy Lynne Holman

No!: My First Book of Protest by Julie Merberg

Enough! 20 Protesters Who Changed America by Emily Easton

A Big Bed for Little Snow by Grace Lin

Black Is a Rainbow Color by Angela Joy, illustrated by Ekua Holmes

Saturday by Oge Mora

Side by Side/Lado a Lado: The Story of Dolores Huerta and Cesar Chavez/La Historia de Dolores Huerta y César Chávez by Monica Brown, illustrated by Joe Cepeda

Sometimes People March by Tessa Allen

We Are Water Protectors by Carole Lindstrom

Your Name Is a Song by Jamilah Thompkins-Bigelow, illustrated by Luisa Uribe

Ganesha's Sweet Tooth by Sanjay Patel and Emily Haynes, illustrated by Sanjay Patel

Monsoon Afternoon by Kashmira Sheth, illustrated by Yoshiko Jaeggi

Little Indians: Stories from Across the Country by Pika Nani, illustrated by Shreya Mehta

Gobble You Up! by Gita Wolf, illustrated by Sunita

The Race for the Chinese Zodiac by Gabrielle Wang

Dim Sum for Everyone! by Grace Lin

Deep in the Sahara by Kelly Cunnane, illustrated by Hoda Hadadi

Shi-shi-etko by Nicola Campbell

Pancho Rabbit and the Coyote: A Migrant's Tale by Duncan Tonatiuh

Young Water Protectors: A Story About Standing Rock by Aslan Tudor and Kelly Tudor

IntersectionAllies: We Make Room for All by Chelsea Johnson, LaToya Council and Carolyn Choi

The Name Jar by Yangsook Choi

Lailah's Lunchbox: A Ramadan Story by Reem Faruqi

Marisol McDonald Doesn't Match/Marisol McDonald no combina by Monica Brown, illustrated by Sara Palacios

Whose Knees Are These? by Jabari Asim, illustrated by LeUyen Pham

Mama's Saris by Pooja Makhijani, illustrated by Elena Gomez

The Rough-Face Girl by Rafe Martin, illustrated by David Shannon

Mangoes, Mischief, and Tales of Friendship: Stories from India by Chitra Soundar

Same, Same But Different by Jenny Sue Kostecki-Shaw

Dear Juno by Soyung Pak

Grandma and the Great Gourd: A Bengali Folktale by Chitra Banerjee Divakaruni, illustrated by Susy Pilgrim Waters

Rattu and Poorie's Adventures in History: 1857 by Parvati Sharma

Brave Ballerina: The Story of Janet Collins by Michelle Meadows, illustrated by Ebony Glenn

Japanese and English Nursery Rhymes: Carp Streamers, Falling Rain and Other Favorite Songs and Rhymes by Danielle Wright

Magic Ramen: The Story of Momofuku Ando by Andrea Wang, illustrated by Kana Urbanowicz

The Gift of Ramadan by Rabiah York Lumbard, illustrated by Laura K. Horton

The Little Red Stroller by Joshua Furst

Leila in Saffron by Rukhsanna Guidroz

Where Are You From? by Yamile Saied Méndez

Not Quite Snow White by Ashley Franklin, illustrated by Ebony Glenn

Sadiq and the Desert Star by Siman Nuurali, illustrated by Anjan Sarkar

Sweet Dreams, Zaza by Mylo Freeman

What Is a Refugee? by Elise Gravel

Fry Bread: A Native American Family Story by Kevin Noble Maillard, illustrated by Juana Martinez-Neal

M Is for Melanin: A Celebration of the Black Child by Tiffany Rose

Freedom Soup by Tami Charles

Bilal Cooks Daal by Aisha Saeed, illustrated by Anoosha Syed

Mommy's Khimar by Jamilah Thompkins-Bigelow

Books for older children

Unstoppable: 75 Stories of Trailblazing Indian Women by Gayathri Ponvannan

Serafina's Promise by Ann E. Burg

Muslim Girls Rise: Inspirational Champions of Our Time by Saira Mir, illustrated by Aaliya Jaleel

For Black Girls Like Me by Mariama J. Lockington

My Life as an Ice Cream Sandwich by Ibi Zoboi, illustrated by Frank Morrison

Planet Omar: Accidental Trouble Magnet by Zanib Mian, illustrated by Nasaya Mafaridik

Karma Khullar's Mustache by Kristi Wientge

My Basmati Bat Mitzvah by Paula J. Freedman

The Whole Story of Half a Girl by Veera Hiranandani

Step Up to the Plate, Maria Singh by Uma Krishnaswami

The Night Diary by Veera Hiranandani

Colorblind: A Story of Racism by Johnathan Harris, art by Donald Hudson

Ruby, Head High: Ruby Bridge's First Day of School by Irène Cohen-Janca

Mango Moon by Diane de Anda

Color Me In by Natasha Díaz

Black Enough: Stories of Being Young & Black in America by Ibi Zoboi and others

The Trouble with Half a Moon by Danette Vigilante

An Indigenous Peoples' History of the United States for Young People by Roxanne Dunbar-Ortiz, adapted by Jean Mendoza and Debbie Reese

An African American and Latinx History of the United States by Paul Ortiz

A Black Woman Did That by Malaika Adero

Because We Can Change the World: A Practical Guide to Building Cooperative, Inclusive Classroom Communities by Mara Sapon-Shevin

Passing for White by Tanya Landman

The Hate U Give by Angie Thomas

A Sky Full of Stars by Linda Williams Jackson

Stella Díaz Has Something to Say by Angela Dominguez

Let the Children March by Monica Clark-Robinson

Can I Touch Your Hair?: Poems of Race, Mistakes, and Friendship by Irene Latham and Charles Waters

Streetcar to Justice: How Elizabeth Jennings Won the Right to Ride in New York by Amy Hill Hearth

Playing Atari with Saddam Hussein by Jennifer Roy with Ali Fadhil

'Daddy Why Am I Brown?': A Healthy Conversation about Skin Color and Family by Bedford Palmer

A Terrible Thing Happened by Margaret Holmes

Just Mercy (Adapted for Young Adults): A True Story of the Fight for Justice by Bryan Stevenson

Being the Change: Lessons and Strategies to Teach Social Comprehension by Sara K. Ahmed

Noughts & Crosses by Malorie Blackman

Orangeboy by Patrice Lawrence

Amazing Grace by Mary Hoffman, illustrated by Caroline Binch

The Civil Rights Movement for Kids: A History with 21 Activities by Mary C. Turck

This Book Is Anti-Racist by Tiffany Jewell

What Is Islamophobia? What Are Hate Crimes and Why Does Faith Matter? and Other Big Questions by Sabeena Akhtar and Na'ima B. Robert

No Turning Back by Beverley Naidoo

Let Me Hear a Rhyme by Tiffany D. Jackson

The Belles by Dhonielle Clayton

Woke: A Young Poet's Call to Justice by Mahogany

L. Browne with Elizabeth Acevedo and Olivia Gatwood

Sita's Ramayana by Samhita Arni, illustrated by Moyna Chitrakar

The Serpent's Revenge: Unusual Tales from the Mahabharata by Sudha Murty

Bronze and Sunflower by Cao Wenxuan, illustrated by Meilo So, translated by Helen Wang

The Boy Who Harnessed the Wind by William Kamkwamba and Bryan Mealer, illustrated by Elizabeth Zunon

Dreaming in Indian: Contemporary Native American Voices by Lisa Charleyboy and Mary Beth Leatherdale

American Born Chinese by Gene Luen Yang

The Thing About Luck by Cynthia Kadohata

Yaqui Delgado Wants to Kick Your Ass by Meg Medina

The Absolutely True Diary of a Part-Time Indian by Sherman Alexie

Malgudi Schooldays by R. K. Narayan

Saving Montgomery Sole by Mariko Tamaki

Mexican Whiteboy by Matt de la Peña

The Library of Fates by Aditi Khorana

The Love and Lies of Rukhsana Ali by Sabina Khan

Watch Us Rise by Renée Watson and Ellen Hagan

Martin & Anne: The Kindred Spirits of Dr. Martin Luther King, Jr. and Anne Frank by Nancy Churnin, illustrated by Yevgenia Nayberg

The Yellow Suitcase by Meera Sriram
Limelight by Solli Raphael
Step Into Your Power: 23 Lessons on How to Live Your Best Life by Jamia Wilson
I Am the Night Sky: & Other Reflections by Muslim American Youth by Next Wave Muslim Initiative Writers
We Are the Change: Words of Inspiration from Civil Rights Leaders by Harry Belafonte
Other Words for Home by Jasmine Warga
Some Places More than Others by Renée Watson
Asha and the Spirit Bird by Jasbinder Bilan

Books for adults

Stamped: Racism, Antiracism, and You by Jason Reynolds and Ibram X. Kendi
Me and White Supremacy: Combat Racism, Change the World, and Become a Good Ancestor by Layla F. Saad
Brit(ish): On Race, Identity and Belonging by Afua Hirsch
Why I'm No Longer Talking to White People About Race by Reni Eddo-Lodge
I Am Not Your Baby Mother by Candice Brathwaite
Sway: Unravelling Unconscious Bias by Pragya Agarwal
Superior: The Return of Race Science by Angela Saini
Natives: Race and Class in the Ruins of Empire by Akala

Afropean: Notes from Black Europe by Johny Pitts

Black and British: A Forgotten History by David
    Olusoga

The Good Immigrant edited by Nikesh Shukla

Brown Baby by Nikesh Shukla

Think Like a White Man by Nels Abbey

Black, Listed by Jeffrey Boakye

*Insurgent Empire: Anticolonial Resistance and British
    Dissent* by Priyamvada Gopal

Partition Voices: Untold British Stories by Kavita Puri

Good Talk: A Memoir in Conversations by Mira Jacob

*The Clapback: Your Guide to Calling Out Racist
    Stereotypes* by Elijah Lawal

Who We Be: The Colorization of America by Jeff
    Chang

Between the World and Me by Ta-Nehisi Coates

*The Warmth of Other Suns: The Epic Story of America's
    Great Migration* by Isabel Wilkerson

The Ordinary Person's Guide to Empire by Arundhati
    Roy

So You Want to Talk About Race by Ijeoma Oluo

*Mixed: An Anthology of Short Fiction on the Multiracial
    Experience,* edited by Chandra Prasad

Your Silence Will Not Protect You by Audre Lorde

The End of Policing by Alex S. Vitale

*Automating Inequality: How High-Tech Tools Profile,
    Police, and Punish the Poor* by Virginia Eubanks

The New Jim Crow: Mass Incarceration in the Age of

Colorblindness by Michelle Alexander
The Fire Next Time by James Baldwin
The Psychology of the Child by Jean Piaget
The Moral Judgement of the Child by Jean Piaget
The Child's Conception of the World by Jean Piaget
Child Psychology and Childhood Education by
   Lawrence Kohlberg
The Psychology of Moral Development by Lawrence
   Kohlberg

Online Listening/Watching
Black Cultural Archives: https://blackculturalarchives.
   org
International Slavery Museum:
   https://www.liverpoolmuseums.org.uk/
   international-slavery-museum
Smithsonian: *Slavery and Freedom* exhibition: https://
   nmaahc.si.edu/slavery-and-freedom
BBC Bitesize: Slavery and its abolition: https://www.
   bbc.co.uk/bitesize/topics/z2qj6sg
BBC *Woman's Hour*: How to talk to your
   children about race and racism:
   http://www.bbc.co.uk/programmes/articles/
   7xvLw6Q4qbJBnkzkj6xm9Z/how-to-talk-to-
   your-children-about-race-and-racism
TED classroom resources about race and racism:
   https://blog.ed.ted.com/2016/07/25/10-ted-
   classroom-resources-about-race-in-america

David Olusoga presents: https://www.youtube.com/
    watch?v=Ut5gtrezN4E
TED talks to understand racism: https://
    www.ted.com/playlists/250/
    talks_to_help_you_understand_r

Podcasts
Outside the Boxes with Pragya Agarwal: https://
    podcasts.apple.com/us/podcast/how-to-talk-
    to-our-children-about-race-and-racism-otb5/
    id1458525955?i=1000447413374
1619 audio series from the *New York Times*: https://
    www.nytimes.com/2019/08/23/podcasts/1619-
    slavery-anniversary.html
NPR *The Race Card Project*: https://www.npr.org/
    series/173814508/the-race-card-project
NPR *Code Switch*: https://www.npr.org/blogs/
    codeswitch
NPR Short Wave 'Understanding Unconscious Bias':
    https://www.npr.org/2020/07/14/891140598/
    understanding-unconscious-bias
About Race with Reni Eddo-Lodge: https://www.
    aboutracepodcast.com
Intersectionality Matters! from The African American
    Policy Forum, hosted by Kimberlé Crenshaw:
    https://aapf.org/podcast
Identity Politics with Ikhlas Saleem and Makkah Ali:
    http://identitypoliticspod.com

No Country for Young Women hosted by Sadia Azmat and Monty Onanuga: https://www.bbc.co.uk/programmes/p063zy3c/episodes/player

Seeing White from Duke University Center for Documentary Studies, hosted by John Biewen: https://www.sceneonradio.org/seeing-white

Groundings hosted by Devyn Springer: https://groundings.simplecast.com

Acknowledgements

This book would not have been possible without my agent Robert Caskie, who believed in me and this book idea and championed it tirelessly, and Sharmaine Lovegrove, my editor and publisher at Dialogue Books, who totally blew me over with her energy and commitment to this project.

The whole team at Little, Brown made this book happen within an unprecedented three months: my wonderful publicist, Millie, along with India, Celeste, David, Thalia and Clare.

I am as ever grateful for Paul, who learns and unlearns every day and fights the good fight with me, parenting with equality, commitment and compassion. In parenting P, I learned and evolved, reflecting on my own ingrained biases. Today she stands up strong and firm, as an ally for those who are marginalised. In parenting I and A, I worry about the world that they are stepping out in, a world that will judge them on the basis of their skin colour, where their identities will be scrutinised and dissected. And so I write this book for them, and for my nephew. They are also the ones who are going to change this world for the better, if we empower them to.

I am also grateful to the many schools, universities and organisations that I have worked with over the years giving workshops and talks for children and adults about race and racism. These conversations gave shape to many of my ideas, while also making me realise how urgent and crucial this book is.

And finally, thank you to all the parents who shared their experiences and questions with me, unafraid of being vulnerable, of making mistakes, of facing their own discomfort. I am so privileged to know you all.

About the Author

Pragya Agarwal is a behavioural and data scientist. After her PhD from University of Nottingham, she was a senior academic in US and UK universities for over 12 years and held the prestigious Leverhulme Fellowship. As well as numerous research papers, Pragya is the author of *Sway: Unravelling Unconscious Bias*, published in 2020. She is also the founder of a research think tank, The 50 Percent Project, examining societal inequities, and a freelance writer for the *Guardian*, *Prospect*, *Forbes*, *Huffington Post*, *BBC Science Focus* and *New Scientist* amongst others. She is currently writing two more books for Canongate.

Pragya is a two-time TEDx speaker and has given keynotes and talks for schools, universities and charities and worked as a consultant with global corporate, governmental and research organisations. Pragya has appeared on many international podcasts and shows such as NPR and *Woman's Hour* and *The Spark* on BBC

Radio 4. She has organised a TEDx Women event and more recently an online South Asian Literary Festival, and has a podcast, *Outside the Boxes*.

Pragya moved to the UK from India almost 20 years ago and now lives in the north-west of England.

Website: www.drpragyaagarwal.com
Twitter: @drpragyaagarwal

Bringing a book from manuscript to what you are reading is a team effort.

Dialogue Books would like to thank everyone at Little, Brown who helped to publish *Wish We Knew What to Say* in the UK.

Editorial
Sharmaine Lovegrove
Thalia Proctor
David Bamford

Contracts
Megan Phillips

Sales
Andrew Cattanach
Ben Goddard
Hannah Methuen
Caitriona Row

Design
Nico Taylor
Jo Taylor

Production
Narges Nojoumi

Publicity
Millie Seaward

Marketing
Emily Moran
Celeste Ward-Best

Copy Editor
Steve Cox
Merlin Cox

Proof Reader
Lydia Cooper